IN THE
HUMAN INTEREST

IN THE
HUMAN
INTEREST
A Strategy to Stabilize
World Population

LESTER R. BROWN

Aspen Institute for Humanistic Studies
Overseas Development Council

W · W · Norton & Company · Inc · New York

ACKNOWLEDGMENTS

Several individuals must be singled out for their special contributions. James P. Grant, president of the Council, strongly supported the notion of an interdisciplinary analysis of the population problem. The generous personal attention of George Brockway, president of W. W. Norton, to this book facilitated its quick publication. Erik Eckholm assisted with the research, but his role went far beyond that as he contributed substantially to the analysis of the problem. The efficiency of Blondeen Duhaney in typing several successive drafts of the manuscript greatly eased the burden of the tight schedule.

Among the many individuals who read and criticized various drafts of the manuscript, often on short notice, are: Bernard Berelson, Harrison Brown, Philander Claxton, Paul Demeny, William Draper, Gail Finsterbusch, Peter Henriot, W. Bert Johnson, Valeriana Kallab, Lawrence Kegan, John Knowles, John Lewis, Robert Muscat, Phyllis Piotrow, Andrew Rice, Ronald Ridker, John Sewell, Davidson Sommers, Michael Teitelbaum, Robert Wallace, and Thomas Wilson. Many have contributed to the evolution of this book, but the conclusions are the author's alone.

Contents

To my children, Brian (age 13) and Brenda (age 7), and others of their generation throughout the world

Foreword

The central issue of our time may well turn out to be how the world addresses the problem of ever expanding human numbers. The world's population may reach the 4 billion mark in 1975 and will not level off, according to the most optimistic projections of the United Nations, until it has reached approximately 10 billion people near the end of the twenty-first century. At the same time, per capita consumption is rising at an even more rapid rate, with the average person's claim on the resources of this finite planet projected to nearly double between the early 1970s and the year 2000.

The prospects are mind-boggling. What would a world be like which contained even 10 billion people, roughly two and a half times as many as today, living at a far more affluent level? For anything approaching 10 billion people to co-exist, staggering changes would be required in the world's political, economic, and social institutions. But will the world act in time to avoid a global catastrophe? The events of 1973, when the crises of food and energy combined to affect significantly virtually all of mankind, are a clear warning that civilization as we know it may not endure until we reach a world of 10 to 16 billion people, each consuming resources at far higher average levels than today.

In the Human Interest, by Lester Brown, concludes that we must stabilize the number of people on this planet at a much lower level (he suggests under 6 billion) than is now generally accepted as possible, and that we must address more urgently the issue of modifying our life styles. He presents the hard policy choices which must be taken by governments if the earth's population is to be stabilized at the lower levels, including the need to increase the motivation for smaller families through increased social and economic progress, and to step up substantially the scale of family planning programs.

This book is a result of an ongoing collaborative process between the Overseas Development Council and the Aspen Institute for Humanistic Studies. For the past three years, the Institute's Program in Environment and Quality of Life has been exploring the interrelationships of environment, energy, population, and resources and their implications for socio-political conflict and for human values. In the summer of 1973, Lester Brown, a Senior Fellow of the Overseas Development Council, was a member of the Core Group of the Program's third international summer workshop, entitled "World Population: The Humanistic Dimension." The Aspen Institute is publishing a summary analysis of the broad political context of the population problem under the authorship of Thomas W. Wilson, Jr., director of its program on environment-related subjects.

In the course of the Aspen workshop, it became clear that the commonly projected patterns of population growth threaten to impose intolerable strains on the world order before population stabilization can be achieved. Lester

Brown's book is intended to re-examine the assumptions on which those projections are based.

In the Human Interest was written with a sense of urgency (indeed, in a matter of months) to enable it to contribute to the global consideration of the population question not only during 1974, which is designated by the United Nations as World Population Year, and at the United Nations Population Conference, scheduled for August 1974, in Bucharest, but also in succeeding years. While possibly no one possesses all the credentials for writing a book with as wide a scope as this one, Lester Brown has earned a deserved reputation in recent years as an analyst who has an unusual ability to see a problem in a broad multi-disciplinary context. It is this multi-disciplinary view of the world population problem that is the intended principal contribution of this book.

The Overseas Development Council is indeed glad to be publishing this book in conjunction with the Aspen Institute. The Council has been interested in the problems of population growth since its inception in 1969—as reflected in the 1973 ODC Monograph, *Smaller Families through Social and Economic Progress,* by former ODC Associate Fellow, William Rich, and in Lester Brown's timely book, *World without Borders,* published in 1972. While the views expressed in this book are those of Lester Brown and do not necessarily represent those of the Council or the Institute, the two institutions are co-sponsoring this book as a significant contribution to the discussion of a most serious problem confronting all mankind.

Finally, we are most appreciative of the financial support from the United Nations Fund for Population Activities. The encouragement from Rafael Salas, executive director of the Fund, and his associate, Tarzi Vittachi, has helped make possible the early publication of this book.

James P. Grant, *President*
Overseas Development Council

IN THE
HUMAN INTEREST

1

Introduction:
A Conceptual Overview

In an increasingly interdependent world the consequences of continuing population growth affect everyone, regardless of where the growth actually occurs. Each person added to the world's population, however poor, exerts an additional claim on the earth's food, energy, and other resources. Expanding food production requires either fossil fuels or animal draft power. It also demands growing quantities of fresh water. Land is required for living space as well as for food production. Even minimal needs for clothing and shelter exert additional claims on the earth's resources.

In an earlier age the addition of another person to the existing world population was of little consequence, since resources far exceeded man's wildest visions of potential needs. The supply of primary commodities exceeded effective demand, resulting in chronically depressed prices and markets highly favorable to buyers. Vast areas of fertile land awaited the plow. Petroleum reserves were greater than envisaged needs. Fresh water was in abundant supply, and the earth's capacity to absorb waste far exceeded man's discharge of waste. The regenerative capacity of forests surpassed man's offtake. There appeared to be more fish in the oceans than man could ever hope to catch.

Suddenly all this is changing. The assumption of boundless abundance of raw materials is being replaced by the prospect of chronic scarcity for many vital ones. World markets for energy and protein are being converted from buyers' to sellers' markets. These and other changes, which became abruptly apparent in the early 1970s, suggest that we may be on the verge of one of the great discontinuities in human history.

Existing projections of economic and demographic trends to the end of the century assume that the final quarter of the century will be largely an extrapolation of the one just ending. We must now question this "business as usual" assumption. During the third quarter of this century, global economic activity tripled, increasing from roughly $1 trillion in 1950 to over $3 trillion in the early 1970s. Existing economic projections call for a repeat of this performance, raising the gross world product to $9 trillion between now and the end of the century. But given the ecological stresses and resource scarcities associated with adding the third trillion dollars to the annual output of goods and services, the addition of another $6 trillion during the final quarter of this century does not now appear likely. The prospect of anything approaching a projected end-of-century population of six and a half billion people must also be reexamined.

Traditionally, the projection of future population growth has been rather exclusively the province of demographers. Differing projections for a given country or continent are the product of modest deviations in assumed fertility behavior and family size. Population growth is customarily treated largely as independent of economic and ecological conditions and the availability of essential resources such as food, energy, and water. But the circumstances in which we now find ourselves suggest that we must radically broaden the framework within which future population prospects are considered. Indeed, that is the purpose of this book.

As of the mid-1970s we know, for example, that energy fuels are in short supply and are likely to become increasingly scarce and costly throughout most of the remainder of the century. Beyond that the prospects are less certain, but most authorities agree that a return to cheap and abundant energy awaits a breakthrough in nuclear fusion power. As the real cost of energy doubles, assumptions governing the future availability of goods and services utilizing energy in their production must be significantly altered.

Information available for the first half of the 1970s reveals some disturbing trends in the world food economy. During the 1970–74 period, the world demand for food, expanded by both population growth and rising affluence, is outstripping world food production. The result is a rapid drawing down of world food reserves, soaring food prices, and growing instability in the world food economy. The nutritional well-being of low-income people throughout the world has been severely and adversely affected by the doubling of world prices of wheat, rice, corn, and soybeans within a two-year span.

The rapid and sustained upward spiral in the world fish catch between 1950 and 1970 appears to have ended abruptly, with the catch shrinking steadily since 1970. If the declining global catch fails to resume an upward trend shortly, this crucial cutback in assumed protein availability will of necessity bear heavily on projections of future population growth. World forest reserves are shrinking as forest land is cleared for other uses and as the demand for wood for fuel, housing, and newsprint exceeds the capacity of forests to renew themselves.

Since 1950, population growth and rising affluence have contributed rather equally to the 4 percent annual growth in global demand for goods and services. Too much time has been spent debating which of the two is more responsible for the resource scarcities and ecological stresses in the world today. It is not one or the other, but both. The debate is wasteful and divisive, since it is usually designed to defend the respective positions of the rich or the poor countries and has shed little light on the issue itself.

Some of the difficulty experienced in assessing the earth's capacity to sustain continuous economic growth derives from the fact that many economists consider ecology a subdiscipline of economics, when in reality the converse may be more accurate. Those of us who are economists forget that the economic structure man has erected rests entirely on the earth's natural resources and processes. Economic activity depends on the earth's capacity to produce food, to absorb waste, to supply fresh water and energy fuels, to produce forest products and fish, and to supply minerals and other raw materials. Without these, there would not be even the most rudimentary economic activities on which man's existence depends.

Another difficulty we face in analyzing and understanding the relationship between population growth and resources is that present and future resource needs are now computed largely at the national level. What is lacking is a systematic effort to sum up projected national needs, relating them to the resources available at the global level at a specified price. Far too little effort has been devoted to analyzing long-term global supply and demand relationships of critical commodities and resources. Acute scarcities have emerged in one resource after another in recent years, often with little warning.

The last few years have witnessed a substantial rise in the level of concern over limits on the earth's resources. The *Limits to Growth* study by the MIT team focused attention on the issues associated with continuous economic and demographic growth.[1] But it created the impression that serious resource scarcities would not occur, at worst, until the early twenty-first century. Within two years after the publication of these projections, we are experiencing a crisis in world fisheries, a steady depletion of global forest resources, an energy crisis, and the prospect that food may be in chronically short supply for the indefinite future.

Growing resource scarcity is contributing to another of the major historical discontinuities of the 1970s. As commodity markets shift from buyers' to sellers' markets, a large measure of political power is shifting from the nations controlling capital and technology toward those controlling raw materials, particularly energy, scarce minerals, and food. The rise to international prominence and influence of major oil exporting nations in 1973 heralded this aspect of the transition into the final quarter of the century.

What we must now recognize is that continuing population growth, even at a moderate rate, will henceforth aggravate virtually all of the important economic, ecological, social, and political problems facing mankind. Population pressure will aggravate problems such as inflation, energy scarcity, food scarcity, and pollution. In the developing world, rural unemployment is rising to alarming levels, generating a massive movement of people from the countryside to cities unprepared for them. One can say with a disturbing degree of confidence that all of these problems will worsen in the absence of a crash effort to slow world population growth.

It is probably safe to say that there are few areas in which the most crucial decision-makers—in this case prospective parents—are so deprived of information on the consequences of their decisions as in that of childbearing. The rate of world population growth is the collective product of hundreds of millions of decisions by individual couples. Most of us understand the short-term consequences of a 3 percent annual rate of population growth in terms of its impact on the need for food, water, housing, education, and other services. But how many of us realize that such a seemingly innocuous rate of growth results in a *nineteenfold increase within a century?* Not only do individual couples contemplating childbearing lack this knowledge and an understanding of its implications for future generations, but so do many national political figures whose leadership in this critical area is essential.

[1]Donella H. Meadows, et al., *The Limits to Growth* (New York: Universe Books, 1972).

No country in the world today can seriously entertain the thought of continuing a population growth rate of 3 percent for an extended period of time. Such an increase within a country of 15 million people, say Algeria, would result in a population of 285 million a century hence. If Indonesia's current population growth rate of 2.7 percent continues for a century, it will result in a population of 1.78 billion, or nearly half the present world population. For anyone who thinks through this one-century scenario, the need to put the brakes on population growth is not only evident and urgent but imperative. The objective of completing the historically witnessed demographic transition as rapidly as possible—i.e., moving from a rapid population growth rate to a moderate rate—no longer suffices. The goal must now become population stabilization—an end to population growth—within every nation of the world.

Just as our formulation of the population problem needs to be broadened, so must our response to it. We can no longer think solely in terms of providing family planning services, critically important though this is. If family planning services are made available, as they should be, to every man and woman throughout the world now deprived of them, population growth rates will be measurably reduced, but this is only one part of the problem. The historical record indicates that human fertility does not usually decline very much unless certain basic social needs are satisfied. Birth rates do not normally drop voluntarily in the absence of an assured food supply, reduced infant mortality rates, literacy, and at least rudimentary health services. In the future, far more attention must be devoted to designing economic and social policies that spread these fundamental improvements in well-being more evenly among national populations, even while the nation is still at a lower level of per capita income. There is growing evidence from societies as diverse as Sri Lanka, Taiwan, China, and Barbados that such policies are possible, and that they help bring down birth rates.

The need is to launch a comprehensive, crash effort to slow population growth quickly, one which encompasses cooperative global efforts both to provide family planning services and to meet the basic social needs of everyone. The population threat is too serious, the required corrective effort too great, to be left to a handful of medical doctors in the Ministry of Health of each developing country. It must now become a concern which encompasses all of society, rich and poor.

The changes required to cope successfully with the population threat are not marginal or trivial. They are fundamental changes that strike at the very structure, functioning, and behavior of society. They challenge many of the fundamental tenets or precepts on which our social and economic systems are based, including the pursuit of superaffluence among the affluent and the desire for large families among the poor. The population threat demands an abrupt alteration of life styles. The near exclusive preoccupation of women with childbearing and rearing, characteristic of many traditional societies, cannot continue for much longer.

The historical discontinuities characterizing the 1970s reflect the need by man to adjust his procreative and consumer behavior and aspirations to the reality of a finite planet. During the third quarter of this century, the overriding emphasis in national economic planning and policy-making has been economic growth—how to expand the supply of goods and services as rapidly as possible. During the concluding quarter of this century, emphasis seems certain to shift from growth to distribution. This is not to say that economic growth will come to a halt but rather that the rate of growth is likely to decline, at least in the more affluent societies. Future efforts to achieve a balance between supply and demand will rely less on expanding supply and more on increasing the efficiency of use of available resources.

No country, however large or wealthy, can any longer view the future security and well-being of its people in isolation. Increasingly, nations will discover that national problems lack national solutions. All countries share a common global ecosystem. National monetary systems are not independent but part of an international monetary system. Activities altering the climate in one part of the world may trigger changes elsewhere, even if inadvertently. Dependence of national economies on international resource flows is rising with each passing year. One small geographic region, the Middle East, controls the lion's share of the world's known reserves of petroleum. North America controls an even larger share of exportable supplies of grains. The interdependence among countries is such that the size of automobiles and level of thermostats in the United States are influenced by oil production and export decisions in the Middle East. Levels of protein intake in Bangladesh, the Soviet Union, and Japan are strongly influenced by U.S. agricultural export decisions.

Where resources are in scarce or fixed supply, we must now face the harsh reality that for some of us to consume more means that others must consume less. Continuing population growth means not only individual hardship and stress but stress on social structures as well. Resource scarcity will often drive up rates of inflation and unemployment, contributing to social and political instability. Scarcity-induced inflation and unemployment will inevitably put great pressure on the international political fabric. The question of how scarce resources are shared among countries may dominate international affairs for decades to come.

At issue is whether we can create a workable world order for an increasingly interdependent world. The role of population policies in that effort could be decisive.

2

Evolution of the Population Problem

Dramatic means have been devised by population growth analysts to alert mankind to the consequences of continuing rapid population growth. Concerned demographers have calculated the time remaining until we reach standing room only. Biologists have calculated the number of centuries until the current 2 percent global rate of population growth would yield a human mass greater than that of the earth itself. One enterprising physicist extended this projection even farther into the future, calculating when the expansion of the human mass would exceed the speed of light.

In this chapter no effort will be made to devise still another way of dramatizing the consequences of continuing population growth. The intent is simply to outline the historical and projected trends in the briefest possible form—to provide a backdrop against which to examine the effect of future population growth on human well-being and security.

Four Demographic Eras

Throughout most of the estimated two million years of man's existence as a distinct species, his numbers were few, measured in the millions. At the time agriculture was developed, some 12,000 years ago, world population probably did not exceed 10 million, no more than the population of London or Iraq today.

At the beginning of the Christian era nearly two millennia ago, world population was estimated at 250 million, almost exactly the same as that of the Soviet Union in 1974. From the beginning of the Christian era until the beginning of the industrial revolution, world population increased to 1 billion. At the beginning of the present century it had reached 1.55 billion. By 1950 it had climbed to 2.5 billion, and in the mid-1970s it is approaching 4 billion.

Man's demographic history appears to divide into four eras—before the discovery of agriculture, from the discovery of agriculture to the onset of the industrial revolution, from the industrial revolution to World War II, and from World War II to the present. The pre-agricultural era, characterized by high death rates and high birth rates, was a very precarious period in man's existence, and by far the longest—it lasted for nearly two million years. Our species might well have disappeared from the face of the earth during this period, except for high fertility levels.

After the invention of agriculture, increases in the food supply contributed to substantial increases in population. As population pressures increased, so did the pressure to innovate in agriculture. Agricultural innovations in turn permitted further increases in population, setting in motion a self-reinforcing cycle that continues until the present. The 12,000 years between the discovery of agriculture and the advent of the industrial revolution were marked by a very slow, though gradually accelerating, rate of population growth.

The industrial revolution accelerated the growth of the world's population not only be creating new economic opportunities but also by spurring advances in industrial technology that further supported the evolution and expansion of agricultural production. By the outbreak of World War II, the increase had reached a new high of just over 1 percent per year.

The burst of scientific ingenuity and economic activity associated with World War II contributed both to substantial increases in the earth's food producing capacity and to dramatic improvements in the capacity to control diseases, ranging from malaria to dysentery. The resulting dramatic reduction in death rates in much of the world created an imbalance between births and deaths unlike any that had ever before existed. Population began to increase at an explosive rate.

Arithmetic of Exponential Growth

The third quarter of the twentieth century has witnessed dramatic alterations in demographic trends, as the global death rate has fallen sharply while the birth rate has remained high. During the first fifteen centuries of the Christian era, world population increased at 2 to 5 percent *per century.* Prior to World War II, few countries had ever experienced a rate of natural increase in excess of 1 percent per year. In some countries today, the rate is between 3 and 4 percent annually, very close to the biological maximum.

Population growth at the rates experienced since World War II are so recent that we have not had adequate time to assess their impact. We need to remind ourselves of the law of exponential growth, and the variation in long-term consequences of even relatively modest population growth rates. A population expanding 1 percent per year increases 270 percent within a century. A population expanding by 3 percent per year multiplies 1,900 percent.

POPULATION INCREASE PER YEAR	POPULATION INCREASE PER CENTURY
(percent)	(percent)
1	270
2	700
3	1,900
4	5,100

The great risk is that mankind will fail to anticipate the consequences of continuous rapid population growth soon enough to curb it before experiencing a global catastrophe of some sort. Even those who are trained in mathematics often fail to appreciate sufficiently the mechanics of exponential growth rates. MIT's *Limits to Growth* study contains a parable that effectively demonstrates the problems associated with exponential population growth on a finite planet. The story is told of a lily pond in which one leaf is growing at the outset. The number of leaves doubles each day, with the result that there are two leaves on the second day, four leaves on the third day, and so on. By the twenty-ninth day, the lily pond is only half full, but on the thirtieth day it is filled completely.

Such is the nature of human population growth on a finite planet. Human beings are the lily leaves and the planet is the pond. A population growing at 1 percent annually increases 2.7 times a century, but raise the rate to 4 percent, which is not a devastating rate of growth for any given year, and it increases fifty-one-fold. Mexico's population, growing at 3.3 percent annually, will increase nearly twenty-six-fold within one century if its growth is not slowed. Its 1970 population of 50 million will reach 1.3 billion in 2070. Similar increases lie ahead for other countries with comparable population growth rates, such as Algeria, Kenya, and the Philippines.

Another way of visualizing the relationship between population growth rates and the absolute increases in population is to calculate the amount of time needed to add a billion people to the earth's population. It took two million years for man's numbers to reach one billion. The second billion came in one hundred years. Successive billions came even faster. At the present rate of increase, the sixth billion will require less than a decade. If the present growth rate were to be maintained until this time next century, it would then take a year to add one billion, and a mere 46 months to add the present world population.

	YEARS REQUIRED TO ADD ONE BILLION PEOPLE	YEAR REACHED
First billion	2,000,000	1830
Second "	100	1930
Third "	30	1960
Fourth "	15	1975
Fifth "	11	1986
Sixth "	9	1995

World population growth is a result of an excess of births over deaths. In 1972, the world crude birth rate (expressed as the number of births per thousand population) was 32; the crude death rate was 13. The excess of births over deaths of 19 per thousand yielded a population growth rate of 1.9 percent annually.

World population increased by 71 million in 1972, the difference between 120 million births and 49 million deaths. Births exceeded deaths by a margin of nearly five to two. Stabilizing population growth requires that the number of births and deaths be brought into balance for the world as a whole.

Two countries, China and India, are now contributing 37 percent of the year-to-year increase in world population. Mainland China's population of 800 million is substantially larger than that of India, but it adds little more to world population, since its birth rate is lower. Some of the comparatively smaller poor countries add more to the world's annual population gain than larger rich ones. Mexico, for example, now contributes much more to the absolute growth in world

population than does the United States. The Philippines adds more
each year than does Japan. Brazil adds 2.8 million additional people
a year, while the Soviet Union adds only 2.2 million.

Table 1. *National Sources of*
World Population Increase, 1972

	MILLIONS
China	13.3
India	12.8
Indonesia	3.4
Brazil	2.8
USSR	2.2
Bangladesh	1.9
Mexico	1.8
Pakistan	1.7
Japan	1.4
Nigeria	1.4
United States	1.3
Philippines	1.3
Thailand	1.1
Iran	1.0
Turkey	1.0
Egypt	.7
Columbia	.7
Ethiopia	.7
Burma	.7
South Korea	.7
All other countries	19.1
TOTAL	71.0

SOURCE: U.S. Agency for International Development.

Structure of the World's Population

The world's population is very unevenly distributed by age groups,
by geographic region, and by income and fertility levels. World population today is a very youthful one. In many less developed countries,
more than 40 percent of the total population is below 15 years of age.
Forty-five percent of the population of Nigeria was below 15 years in

1972; for Brazil the comparable figure was 42 percent, and for Indonesia it was 45.

In societies with such an age structure, the youth dependency ratio —the proportion of youth to economically active adults—is very high. Half the people in the less developed world are below 19 years of age. This contrasts with a median age of 31 for the more developed countries, where the population is much more evenly distributed by age group. At the other end of the age spectrum, the elderly dependency ration—the proportion of those over 65 to the economically active population—is much lower. Within the developing countries it is only 3 percent, while in the developed countries it is nearly 11 percent. In both, the dominant source of dependence on the working segment consists of those too young to work rather than those too old to do so.

Geographic distribution is at least as uneven as age distribution. More than half of the world's people live in Asia. The remaining half is rather evenly distributed among the other five geographic regions: Western Europe, North America, Latin America, Africa, and Eastern Europe, including the Soviet Union. Population within these regions ranges from 230 million in North America to 380 million in Africa.

The global distribution of people is determined not only by land area but also, importantly, by the availability of water. In this respect most of Asia is rather richly endowed. It is the monsoon climate, high rainfall, and annual flooding of river plains that makes possible the extensive wet rice cultivation which sustains such an enormous concentration of people.

Differences among national populations in fertility levels are great. Crude birth rates may range from above 50 in some less developed countries to below 15 in several industrial societies. The result is a world in which population size has stabilized in some societies while it is increasing at a rate of thirtyfold per century in others.

A majority of the world's population is rural. In some of the larger less developed countries, such as India and China, close to four-fifths of the people live in rural areas. These rural-urban proportions are almost exactly reversed in highly urbanized societies, such as the United Kingdom, Belgium, or Japan.

Economic variations are also dramatic. One-third of all the people in the world live in countries that have average annual incomes below $100 per year. Well over half live in countries with incomes below $200 per year. In some of the industrial societies, average incomes are now several thousand dollars per year. The average income in the United States, Japan, or West Germany may be 40 times that in India, Ethiopia, or Bolivia.

UN Population Projections

United Nations projections of population to the end of the century show three alternative levels of population in the year 2000—6 billion, 6.5 billion, and 7.1 billion. The middle-level projection, viewed by the UN demographers as the most likely, assumes a world population growth rate of 2 percent until 1985, followed by a gradual decline to 1.7 percent by the end of the century. The low and high projections reflect corresponding variations in assumed growth rates.

The United Nations has very usefully projected world population growth beyond the end of the century, extrapolating the three alternative trends until world population eventually stabilizes. The essential assumptions common to the three population projections are that fertility in all regions will eventually decline to replacement levels and that once at replacement it will hold there for several decades until population stabilizes. Replacement level fertility is that level which enables couples to replace themselves—in effect, two children per couple. In reality, it must be slightly greater than two in order to allow for the small number of infants who do not reach reproductive age.

The disturbing finding is how long it will take to reach population stability under these assumptions. Even under the "low" variant, population does not stabilize until near the end of the twenty-first century, at just under 10 billion. Under the "medium" variant, the one referred to by UN demographers as "relatively optimistic," stability is reached in 2125, when population reaches 12.3 billion. The "high" variant projects population stability in 2135, at 16 billion.

The differences between the three projections are accounted for largely by variations in the time frame in which nations are assumed to reach replacement level fertility. The medium projections assume that all regions will achieve replacement level fertility between 2010 and 2065, with the most developed nations reaching this level first and the less developed regions later. The high projections assume this

Table 2. United Nations Alternative
Projections of World Population

	1970	2000	2050	2150
		(billions)		
Low	3.6	6.0	9.2	9.8
Medium	3.6	6.5	11.2	12.3
High	3.6	7.1	13.8	16.0

would occur for each region ten years later than the medium projections, and the low projections assume it would be achieved ten years sooner. Even under the low assumption, world population nearly triples, continuing to grow for another century and a quarter. Population in the less developed countries reaches 7.9 billion under the low assumption and 14.1 billion under the high!

The explicit assumptions underlying these alternative projections are almost exclusively demographic in nature. They deal with such matters as fertility behavior and life expectancy. They do not examine the effect of these various population levels, supported at acceptable levels of consumption, on the amount of waste generated, the extent of pressure on ocean fisheries, the amount of energy this would require, the thermal pollution it would generate, the stress on food producing ecosystems, or the level of unemployment. Stated another way, the ecological, economic, social, and political stresses associated with these enormous projected increases in population are not taken into account. If these are considered, then even the "low" projection of just under 10 billion people becomes unrealistic.

Part II *POPULATION GROWTH ON
A FINITE PLANET*

3

Population, Affluence,
and Economic Growth

Political leaders in the rich countries are quick to blame rapid population growth for many problems mankind faces today, particularly
those of environmental stress and resource scarcity. Political leaders
in the poor countries counter with the charge that rising per capita
consumption by the affluent is at the root of resource shortages. Both
are right, but a meaningful answer must be much more specific.

Population versus Affluence

The growth in world output of goods and services has averaged 4
percent per year since 1950. Since we know that the world's population
has been growing at roughly 2 percent annually, we can conclude that
it absorbed about half of the increase in the global growth of goods
and services produced during this period. The remainder, also about
2 percent, must have been absorbed by rising individual affluence. In
a general way, then, we know that population growth and rising
affluence have each generated half of the world growth in demand for
goods and services since mid-century. Although the growth in over-all
demand generated by population growth and by rising affluence are
roughly equal at the global level, they vary widely between the poor
and rich countries. Within the poor countries, it is population growth

that has absorbed the lion's share of the increase in production. Within the rich countries, rising affluence has been the dominant factor.

Beyond these broad generalizations, one cannot argue very definitively about which is the more important source of additional demand except in relation to certain specific commodities. And even then, as the following discussion of food illustrates, precise statements can be made only on a country-by-country basis.

During the 1960s, the food problem was perceived at the global level primarily as a food/population problem, a race between food and people. At the end of each year, observers anxiously compared increases in food production with those of population to see if any progress was being made. During the 1970s, rapid global population growth continues to generate demand for more food but, in addition, rising affluence is emerging as a major new claimant on world food resources. Historically, there was only one important source of growth in world demand for food; there are now two.

At the global level, population growth still accounts for most of the increasing demand for food. If world population continues to expand at nearly 2 percent per year, doubling in little more than a generation, merely maintaining current consumption levels will also require a doubling of food production.

The effect of rising affluence on the world demand for food is perhaps best understood by examining its effect on grain requirements. Grain consumed directly provides 52 percent of man's food energy supply; consumed indirectly in the form of livestock products, it provides a significant share of the remainder. In resource terms, grains occupy more than 70 percent of the world's cropland.

In the poor countries, the annual availability of grain per person averages only about 400 pounds per year, or just over one pound per day. Nearly all of this small amount must be consumed directly to meet minimum energy needs; little can be spared for conversion into animal protein. In the United States and Canada, per capita grain utilization is currently approaching one ton per year. Of this total, only about 150 pounds are consumed directly in the form of bread, pastries, and breakfast cereals; the remainder is consumed indirectly in the form of meat, milk, and eggs. The agricultural resources—land, water, fertilizer—required to support an average North American are nearly five times those required for the average Indian, Nigerian, or Colombian (see Table 3).

Throughout the world, per capita grain requirements rise with income. The amount of grain consumed directly rises until per capita income approaches $500 per year, whereupon it begins to decline, eventually leveling off at about 150 pounds. The total amount of grain consumed directly and indirectly, however, continues to increase rapidly as per capita income climbs. As yet, no nation appears to have reached a level of affluence where its per capita grain requirements have stopped rising.

Throughout the developing world, of course, population growth accounts for most of the growth in the demand for food. Only very limited progress is being made, and only in some countries, in raising per capita consumption. In the more affluent nations, on the other hand, rising income accounts for most of the growth. In Japan and France, for example, where population is growing at about 1 percent per year and per capita incomes at several percent annually, growth in the demand for food derives principally from rising affluence.

Wherever population has stopped growing, as in West Germany, all the increase in domestic food supplies can be used to upgrade diets. In a country such as India, however, where income rises are scarcely perceptible and population continues to expand rapidly, the burgeon-

Table 3. *Annual Per Capita Grain Consumption in Selected Nations 1964–66 Average*

	GRAIN CONSUMED DIRECTLY, INCLUDING BREAD, PASTRIES, AND BREAKFAST CEREALS	GRAIN CONSUMED INDIRECTLY AS MEAT, MILK, AND EGGS	TOTAL GRAIN CONSUMED	TOTAL GRAIN CONSUMED AS MULTIPLE OF INDIAN CON- SUMPTION
	(pounds)	(pounds)	(pounds)	
Canada[a]	152	1,696	1,848	5
United States	143	1,343	1,486	4
USSR	344	883	1,227	4
United Kingdom	169	856	1,025	3
Argentina	223	625	848	2
West Germany	160	588	748	2
Mexico	305	242	547	2
Japan	320	211	531	2
China	312	118	430	1
India	288	60	348	1

SOURCE: FAO, *Food Balance Sheets, 1964–66 Average.*
[a]1959–61 average

ing demand for food derives almost completely from population growth. In Brazil, which has had rapid growth in both population and per capita income, both factors loom large.

From the beginning of agriculture until World War II, year-to-year increases in the demand for food had been almost entirely the result of population growth; only in the postwar period, and particularly since the late 1960s, has rising affluence emerged as a major claimant on world food resources. Of the current 30-million-ton average annual growth in world grain output, an estimated 22 million tons is absorbed by population growth and 8 million tons by rising per capita incomes.

After food, no resource is more essential to modern society than energy. Worldwide, the use of energy is expanding by nearly 6 percent a year—three times as fast as population. Many developing countries, especially those in which the industrial sector is growing rapidly and from a small base, are increasing energy consumption even faster than affluent societies such as the United States, where growth has been about 4 percent per year. Yet differing rates of growth in national energy consumption should not obscure the vast variation in per capita energy consumption in countries at different income levels.

Variations in the consumption of food are bounded on the lower end by the minimum required for human survival and on the upper end by the dimensions of the human stomach. Even with a diet high in animal protein, the variation among countries in per capita agricultural resource requirements is not likely to exceed five to one. This contrasts sharply with energy, where variations are vast. Consumption of modern energy fuels (fossil, nuclear, and hydroelectric) by the average American in 1971 was 191 times that of the average Nigerian (see Table 4). It was 351 times that of the average Ethiopian.

This comparison dramatizes the fact that modern man is an enormous consumer of energy, depending on it for mobility (automobiles, trucks, planes, trains, ships, elevators), for manufacturing material goods of all kinds, for producing food (fertilizers, plowing, harvesting, milking cows), for light, for heat (homes or food preparation), for cooling (refrigerating, freezing, air conditioning), and even for thinking (calculators and computers). In a modern economy, moreover, petroleum and its derivatives constitute the basic raw material for the manufacture of a wide range of goods ranging from plastics to pesticides to synthetic fibers.

In contrast, the subsistence farmer in a pre-industrial society produces the food he needs through his own energies and those of his draft animals. He does not require energy for the production process beyond that provided by sunlight and photosynthesis for the food he and his animals must eat. If the goods and amenities available to him

Table 4. *Per Capita Energy Consumption, 1971*
(15 most populous nations)

COUNTRY	KG. PER CAPITA (coal equivalent)[a]	ENERGY USE AS MULTIPLE OF NIGERIAN USE
United States	11,244	191
United Kingdom	5,507	93
West Germany	5,223	89
USSR	4,535	77
France	3,928	67
Japan	3,267	55
Italy	2,682	45
Mexico	1,270	22
China	561	10
Brazil	500	8
Philippines	298	5
India	186	3
Indonesia	123	2
Pakistan (incl. Bangladesh)	96	2
Nigeria	59	
World average	1,927	33

SOURCE: *UN Statistical Yearbook,* 1972.
[a]Includes coal, lignite, petroleum, natural gas, hydro and nuclear electricity.

are limited to those he can produce with his own hands, firewood may constitute his only other energy need.

In nations with rapidly growing populations and slowly growing economies, per capita energy use is increasing only very slowly. Rapid population growth necessitates large increases in total energy consumed nationally, but just to maintain past levels of per capita consumption. Per capita energy consumption in India is growing at less than 1 percent yearly, for example, scarcely one-fourth as fast as in the United States. In Japan, a country with extremely rapid economic growth and slow population growth, more than nine-tenths of the annual increase in national energy consumption is used to raise individual consumption.

World consumption of all mineral ores has been increasing rather steadily throughout this century, with the pattern interrupted only by an acceleration during the two world wars and a downturn during the

Depression. Excluding these exceptions, the trends of increase are remarkably regular. If the period that has been required for consumption to double is used as a measure, these are found to be short: 9 years for aluminum; 10 to 15 years for iron; 12 to 15 years for copper; 17 years for zinc; and 20 years for lead. The doubling time for these minerals is so much less than the 36-year doubling time of world population that affluence must of necessity account for much of the growth in their demand.

The principal exceptions are those minerals used primarily for chemical fertilizer, particularly phosphates and potash. Here the source of growth in demand is essentially the same as for food, where population dominates.

World mineral consumption is dominated by the United States, which now uses from one-fifth to one-third of most minerals. In per capita terms, Americans, Europeans, and Japanese consume perhaps 20 times as much metallic ore as the average person in the poorer countries (see Table 5). If consumption in these countries should ever begin to approach levels prevailing in the rich ones, the adequacy of supplies, particularly of the scarcer minerals, would quickly become a matter of concern.

As consumption rises and reserves are depleted, uncertainty over the future supply of certain minerals is rising. The more accessible supplies in those countries that industrialized earliest are being worked out to the point where further mining becomes very expensive. The search therefore shifts to new sources of supply, and to possible substitutes.

Even renewable resources are being depleted. As a result of both the steady global growth in consumption of forest products and of the expansion of agriculture, residential and industrial development, and highway networks, the earth is gradually being deforested. The seemingly insatiable demand for forest products coupled with the gradual reduction of forested area presents us with the classic problem of exponential growth in demand pressing against a shrinking resource base. In the less developed countries, population growth generates additional demands for wood for fuel to be used for cooking and heating. Although the use of wood for fuel is reduced when rising incomes permit the substitution of other fuels, the amount of forest products used for construction and furniture climbs rapidly. In addition, the progressive spread of literacy in the developing countries increases the demand for newsprint.

The supply-demand relationship for forest products is closely related to the demand for energy and food. In many developing countries, the local use of wood for fuel is exceeding the regenerative

Table 5. *Steel Consumption Per Capita, 1971*
(15 most populous nations)

	KG. PER CAPITA	STEEL CONSUMPTION AS MULTIPLE OF INDONESIAN CONSUMPTION
United States	617	123
West Germany	580	116
Japan	551	110
USSR	471	94
France	414	83
United Kingdom	361	72
Italy	339	68
Mexico	78	16
Brazil	77	15
China	31	6
Philippines	21	4
India	14	3
Nigeria	10	2
Pakistan (incl. Bangladesh)	6	1
Indonesia	5	1
World average	155	31

SOURCE: *UN Statistical Yearbook, 1972.*

capacity of local forests, forcing a shift to the use of kerosene or other fuel. As the global demand for food rises, land is shifted from forestry to agriculture. The cumulative effect of this trend is growing global scarcity of lumber and paper.

Energy and Economic Growth

Energy is available to man in various forms, ranging from sunlight to controlled nuclear reactions to coal and oil. The critical energy scarcities being confronted in the 1970s do not reflect a long-run shortage of energy per se, but rather a scarcity of the cheaper and easily usable forms of energy. In the case of petroleum, the concentration of exportable supplies in relatively few locations has made possible restrictions on supply growth and price competition. As the world's scientists and politicians ponder various technological responses to the energy crisis, awareness has been heightened of the element of convenience that has made us so dependent on such fossil fuels as oil and natural gas. These products are easy to extract, easy to transport, and simple to utilize. In addition, the environmental side effects of extraction and use are considerably less damaging than those of coal—a major alternative source of energy. These factors explain why oil and natural gas together supplied four-fifths of the energy consumed in the United States by 1973, with oil alone supplying half.

The extremely rapid rate of growth in worldwide energy consumption has been made possible by the ready availability of relatively inexpensive energy supplies. If global consumption were to continue to rise at recent rates, total annual world energy requirements at the end of the century would be 4.5 times the 1973 level. Clearly, however, the world will not be able in the coming decades to sustain this growth rate.

Growth in energy consumption will be restricted both by the increasingly high prices of commodities such as petroleum and natural gas resulting from the exercise of bargaining power by exporters, and by the higher cost of alternate energy sources being developed. The long lead times involved in the development and dissemination of new technologies and sources of energy mean that the total volume of energy which would be required for a continuing consumption growth rate of 6 percent simply may not be forthcoming at any feasible price for at least two decades, and possibly longer.

A combination of factors—the scarcity of energy supplies in relation to demand, energy prices considerably higher than those of the past, and the massive capital investments required to open up new energy sources—will necessitate major changes in the rate and pattern of economic growth in both rich and poor nations. Individual life styles in nations with high per capita energy consumption will be altered substantially.

Economic growth during the past quarter century has depended heavily on rapidly expanding supplies of petroleum. Western Europe's annual growth in gross national product (GNP) of 4.4 percent in the late 1960s, for example, was associated with a 7 percent annual growth in oil consumption. Japan's annual economic growth of 12.4 percent in that period was accompanied by a 17.5 percent rate of increase in oil consumption. The North American economy grew at an annual rate of 3.7 percent from 1965 to 1970, and oil consumption climbed by 4.9 percent.

The countries whose future economic growth is most threatened are the poorer countries which must import a large share of their energy requirements. If already scarce foreign exchange and potential investment capital must be devoted more and more to paying the rising energy import bill covering minimal basic needs of the population, prospects for any real growth of the nascent industrial and modern agricultural sectors will be seriously jeopardized.

Domino Effect of Resource Scarcity

The traditional economic response to resource scarcity has been the substitution of another material for that which is in short supply. Thus when copper prices rose above a certain level, industrialists throughout the world gave increasing attention to substituting aluminum or other metals for copper in their manufacturing processes. When fish meal was in short supply, farmers could replace it with soybean meal in their poultry and pig feed rations.

Substitution of a less scarce resource for a more scarce one is economically logical, and when shortages exist for only a few products it is a relatively easy way to avoid any seriously detrimental impact from resource shortages. But in a world where many key resources are becoming increasingly scarce, substitution can rarely serve as a panacea for the shortage of any one commodity. Instead, the opportunities for substitution frequently ensure only that scarcity will be highly contagious.

Often, in fact, a domino effect of resource scarcity is in operation. The rising price of petrochemicals with which to produce synthetic fibers puts added pressures on the supply of natural fibers. The resulting scarcity of natural fibers in turn pulls American cropland needed for soybean production into cotton production, further aggravating the world protein shortage. The scarcity of water in the vicinity of the coal fields in northeastern Wyoming poses serious constraints on efforts to establish large-scale coal gasification plants, thus aggravating the energy crisis. The list of such extended chains or networks of resource interdependence is virtually endless.

This domino effect may frequently have significant international economic ramifications. In early 1974, the shortage of energy in Japan was causing a serious cutback in the production of chemical fertilizers. Japan in turn reduced its exports of fertilizers even though it is an important supplier for many Asian nations. In such nations as India, the Philippines, and Indonesia, a significant fall in fertilizer imports will almost certainly lead to a drop in food production, thus raising the need to import food commodities at a time when they are already in short global supply.

Technological Fixes

The three decades from 1940 to 1970 were marked by unprecedented scientific and technological advances in virtually all fields of scientific and economic activity, ranging from agriculture to solid state physics. The impressive array of advances, from splitting the atom to development of high-yield wheats and transistor radios, culminated in the landing of Americans on the moon in 1969. It gave rise to an unbounded confidence in the capacity of technology to solve problems and fulfill needs. The "technological fix" was becoming an integral part of our view of the future. Shortages of energy fuels would be overcome by development of additional reserves or alternative energy sources. If protein was in short supply, it would be manufactured. During the 1970s, however, this confidence in technological quick fixes has been badly shaken.

Over the past quarter century, the expansion of electrical power supplies through the use of nuclear reactors has received strong support from governments and the scientific community as a means of reducing pressures on energy supplies. However, unsolved problems of safety, waste disposal, and thermal pollution have resulted in substantial opposition to the rapid spread of nuclear fission power plants by major elements of the public and the scientific community and by local governments. These fears, combined with continuing technical and economic problems, have resulted in a much slower expansion of nuclear power than advocates had hoped. By 1973, less than 1 percent of the energy consumed in the United States, and less than 2 percent of that consumed worldwide, was generated in nuclear plants.

As a result of the crisis atmosphere regarding energy issues that mushroomed in 1973, the expansion of nuclear fission power facilities is being stepped up in many nations. But the opposition to their rapid spread remains and is likely to continue to retard future development. One hundred top world scientists gathered at the twenty-third annual Pugwash Conference on Science and World Affairs, meeting in Aulanko, Finland, in the fall of 1973, jointly declared: "The as yet unsolved problem of waste management and the possibly unsolvable (in an absolute sense) problems of catastrophic releases of radioactivity and diversion of bomb-grade material, combine to create grave and justified misgivings about the vast increase in the use of nuclear power that has been widely predicted. The wisdom of such an increase must at the present time be seriously questioned."

In any case, any conceivable rate of expansion of nuclear power plants will not be sufficient to eliminate energy supply problems in the next three decades if demand continues its recent upward course. Amory Lovins of the Massachusetts Institute of Technology, calculating world energy needs in the year 2000 on the basis of an assumed growth rate of 5 percent (slightly lower than the growth rate of the 1970s), observes: "If we could somehow build one huge nuclear power station per day for the rest of this century, starting today, then when we were through, more than half our primary energy would still come from fossil fuels, which would be consumed about twice as fast as now."

Over the longer term, it is hoped that the harnessing of nuclear fusion—the process that powers the sun and the thermonuclear bomb —will provide a far safer source of energy without the resource constraints of fission reactors, which must be supplied with uranium, an increasingly scarce commodity. Scientists can now see at least the theoretical possibility of a fusion process which would not be accompanied by the threat of an uncontrolled explosion or radioactive leaks. As of 1974, no one is absolutely certain that a fusion reactor power plant will ever be possible; but if the expanded research efforts of the next two decades pay off, some experts believe that a commercial prototype might be available before the end of the century. Even so, the diffusion of this extraordinarily complex technology would presumably not be a rapid process.

A third nuclear alternative, the fast breeder reactor, is currently receiving close study, since it generates more nuclear fuel than it consumes. Breeder reactors may involve environmental and safety problems at least as great as those of the fission reactor, however, and their economic feasibility remains speculative.

The development of new and alternative energy sources in the years to come will exact a heavy price from societies, both in capital investments required and in the inevitable environmental trade-offs. The United States and Canada have vast reserves of oil-bearing shale and tar sands from which petroleum can be extracted, and coal from which natural gas can be manufactured. But the investments required to set up such operations on a continentally significant scale will dwarf past investments in oil and gas drilling.

In addition, extensive strip mining in some of the most scenic areas of the North American continent will be necessary to extract the shale, tar, and coal. Beyond this, waste disposal problems that now seem insuperable would be created by large-scale production of oil from shale. Each barrel of oil extracted will leave more than a ton of waste residue to be disposed of somehow, whether by filling valleys or creating new mountains of waste to complement the Rocky Mountain skyline. It is not at all clear that a majority of Americans will be willing to pay such heavy environmental costs even if the capital needed for major shale, tar, and coal gasification development is forthcoming.

Production of petroleum from oil shale may be severely limited in any case by the lack of water in the areas of Colorado, Utah, and Wyoming where most high-quality shale is located. From 100 to 170 million gallons of water would be required daily by a plant producing 1 million barrels of shale oil per day. Unfortunately, the limited water resources of the upper Colorado region are already heavily committed to agriculture and residential use. The President's National Commission on Materials Policy reported in mid-1973 that "ultimately, surface water supplies may limit the size of the shale oil industry to perhaps 3 or 5 million barrels of production per day." This total would constitute an important addition to U.S. energy supplies—but would still constitute less than the projected *increase* in U.S. energy imports between 1973 and 1980. And it assumes that the 4 to 7 million tons of solid waste generated *daily* could be disposed of in an acceptable manner.

One response to petroleum scarcity in the United States has been an increase in the use of coal, the most abundant fossil fuel, to heat buildings and produce electricity. Providing the added coal supplies is requiring an increase in strip mining, and the burning of coal pollutes the air more than natural gas or oil. The incidence of respiratory diseases and eye irritations in urban communities may rise as a result. In several western states, low-sulfur coal, which would reduce air pollution, can be extracted by strip mining. Often, however, sufficient water may not be available to restore the decimated land.

Even the tapping of major new petroleum finds is proving to involve costs far greater than those our economy and habits are accustomed to bearing. The costs of producing a barrel of oil in the relatively recently discovered oil fields in the North Sea, the north slope of Alaska, and Siberia are far higher than those in the Texas-Oklahoma oil fields or the Persian Gulf.

More exotic proposals, such as the massive harnessing of geothermal, solar, tidal, or wind power, are receiving increasing attention. None of these is likely to prove economically attractive on a large scale in the foreseeable future, however. Given what we know about the lead times involved in developing and utilizing new technologies in the energy field, there is little chance of a breakthrough in energy sources that will permit a return to cheap energy before 1990 at the earliest—and quite possibly much farther into the future.

Over the last decade, numerous non-conventional techniques have been set forth for expanding the world food supply. Many have been exceedingly interesting from a technological point of view, but few have materialized in the way their proponents had hoped. New foods must be not only technologically possible but also economically feasible and, most important, people must be willing to eat them.

Among the proposals was one for the use of less desirable species of fish to produce fish protein concentrate, which could be added to various conventional dishes to provide a low-cost method of increasing protein intake and improving nutrition. Some technological problems with the process remain unsolved, and as of 1974 it is receiving relatively little attention either in the scientific community or among food processors.

A second widely discussed possibility for augmenting human food supplies involves the use of single-celled microorganisms, principally certain strains of yeast, to convert petroleum or other organic materials into edible forms of protein. This process was at one time being actively researched by twenty-six international oil companies in various parts of the world. The hopes for this process have not yet materialized on a significant scale, though a few commercial plants are being constructed. British Petroleum, the leader in this field, has been operating a small pilot plant in France, and has future plans for producing as much as 100,000 tons of protein for animal feed annually. Some single cell protein (SCP) is also being produced in the Soviet Union, though data on how much are not available. The plans of two Japanese chemical firms to produce a total of 150,000 tons yearly for animal feed were recently scrapped, primarily because of extreme resistance on the part of Japanese consumers, who suspected that even the indirect consumption of SCP might not be medically safe.

Technical problems in the production of SCP have proved to be formidable, and clearance for marketing has been achieved only for feed-grade protein to be used in livestock feed. Serious problems must yet be overcome before this protein can safely be consumed directly by human beings. Beyond this, the rising price of petroleum requires a wholly new assessment of the economic feasibility of large-scale production.

During the 1960s, many proposed the use of algae on a massive scale as a source of nutritious food. To date, however, both cost and palatability problems with algae products remain to be overcome. Meanwhile, pilot projects and experimentation are under way in numerous other areas, including the improvement of fish farming techniques, the recycling of animal wastes, and nutritional improvements of various grain varieties. Research in all such areas should continue and deserves strong support. There is little likelihood, however, that any such advancements will have a significant impact on global food supplies before the end of this decade. Beyond that point the prospects are uncertain.

Nuclear power advocates attempted during the mid-1960s to relate to the world food crisis by proposing that nuclear power be used to operate gigantic desalting complexes, which would be sited in desert areas close to the oceans. These nuclear-powered agro-industrial complexes, it was argued, could measurably increase the world food supply if they could be made economically practicable. With growth in nuclear power throughout the world falling farther and farther behind schedule, and the cost of other energy sources rising, this cannot be regarded as a promising avenue in the foreseeable future.

Energy and food are not the only resources plagued by scarcity for which quick and easy technological fixes are lacking. The shortage of forest products can be partially alleviated through the planting of faster-growing tree varieties, but this is a relatively slow process involving decades. When minerals such as copper and bauxite become scarce, it is frequently feasible to open up mining operations in sites with lower-grade ore as the price of the ore rises. But low-grade ore mining operations are usually both extremely energy intensive and ecologically disruptive, and the high cost of energy may reduce substantially the attractiveness of this option.

The preceding discussion is not intended to be anti-technology; rather, it seeks to put the difficulties we face into perspective. One can argue that the need for new technologies may be at least as important in the future as in the past. But the emphasis in research and development will shift from the expansion of resource supplies to greater efficiency in resource use. A dramatic example of a technology that resulted in more efficient resource use was Intelsat's first transatlantic communications satellite *Early Bird.* Weighing only 85 pounds, it carried a communications load equivalent to that of 100,000 tons of transoceanic cable. In addition, it was solar powered. The high-yield wheats and rices that underlie the Green Revolution also represent quantum jumps in the efficiency of resource use. They produce 50 to 100 percent more grain per unit input of land, water, labor, and fertilizer. It is on this type of resource conserving technology that scientists must increasingly focus their energies.

Growth Prospects in a World of Scarcity

The emergence of serious resource scarcities and severe ecological stresses during the early 1970s calls into question economic growth prospects for the final quarter of this century. Most existing projections of economic growth are now obsolete, simply because many assumptions on which they are based, especially an abundant supply of low-cost energy, are no longer valid. A slowing in the growth in output of goods and services may lead to intense competition between population growth and rising affluence for available goods and resources, both within and among societies. In effect, the competition will be between the subsistence requirements of a rising population curve and the strong desire on the part of those with superior purchasing power to raise their levels of consumption.

Traditional economic relationships between rich countries and poor will be altered. Until recently, a positive relationship has existed between economic growth rates in the rich countries and in the poor. The more rapidly the former grew, the greater the opportunities for the latter to expand their exports and economic output. In the age of scarcity, however, continuing rapid growth in consumption of scarce resources in the rich countries could jeopardize economic growth in the poor ones. Massive Soviet imports of wheat have helped raise the world price, thereby depriving many developing countries of needed supplies of a dietary staple. And the massive and growing energy imports into the United States, already consuming more energy per capita than any other country, may seriously hinder economic growth prospects in those developing countries that are also energy importers.

For the first time in modern economic history, the world is moving into a situation where, with certain of the scarcer resources, the consumption of more by some necessarily means the consumption of less by others. This raises the critical political issue of how scarce resources will or should be shared among people with widely varying purchasing power. It also suggests the need to end the unrestrained pursuit of superaffluence. At a minimum, the economic circumstances now prevailing in the world suggest a dramatic reorientation of both economic goals and demographic policies and programs.

4

Growing Pressure on
World Food Resources

As of the mid-1970s, it has become apparent that the soaring demand for food, spurred by both population growth and rising affluence, has begun to outrun the productive capacity of the world's farmers and fishermen. The result is declining food reserves, skyrocketing food prices, and increasingly intense international competition for exportable food supplies.

We have entered an era in which global grain reserves, which provide a crucial measure of safety when crop failures occur, are likely to remain on the low side, and in which little, if any, excess cropland will be held idle under farm programs in the United States. Food prices are likely to remain high, placing a special burden on the world's poor.

Since the invention of agriculture roughly 12,000 years ago, the earth's food-producing capacity has increased several hundredfold. Yet hunger has remained the lot of a large segment of humanity. Now food price inflation is helping to undermine the prosperity and economic stability of the well-fed countries as well. At issue today is whether or not man can break the dismal cycle in which increased food production has been largely absorbed by an ever growing population.

Affluence and the Demand for Food

As noted in the previous chapter, rising incomes as well as population growth are generating a rapid growth in the demand for food supplies. The impact of rising affluence on the consumption of livestock products is evident in trends in the United States over the past generation. For example, per capita consumption of beef climbed from 55 pounds in 1940 to 116 pounds in 1972, more than doubling. Poultry consumption rose from 18 pounds to 51 pounds during the same period.

There is now a northern tier of industrial countries—beginning with the United Kingdom in the west and including Scandinavia, Western Europe, Eastern Europe, the Soviet Union, and Japan—whose dietary habits more or less approximate those of the United States in 1940. As incomes continue to rise in this group of countries containing some two-thirds of a billion people, a sizable fraction of the additional income is being converted into demand for livestock products, particularly beef. Many of these countries, such as Japan and those in Western Europe, are densely populated; others, the Soviet Union for example, suffer from a scarcity of fresh water. Because they lack the capacity to satisfy the growth in demand for livestock products entirely from indigenous resources, they are importing increasing amounts of either livestock products or feed grains and soybeans with which to expand their livestock production.

New Constraints on Protein Supplies

At a time when rising affluence is manifesting itself in the form of rapidly growing demand for high-quality protein, we suddenly find ourselves in difficulty in our efforts to rapidly expand the supplies of three major protein sources—beef, soybeans, and fish.

There are two major constraints on beef production. Agricultural scientists have not been able to devise any commercially satisfactory means of getting more than one calf per cow per year; for every animal that goes into the beef production process, one adult animal must be fed and otherwise maintained for a full year. There does not appear to be any prospect of an imminent breakthrough on this front. The other constraint on beef production is good grassland. The grazing capacity of much of the world's pastureland is now almost fully utilized. This is true, for example, in much of the U.S. Great Plains area, in large areas of sub-Saharan Africa, and in parts of Australia. There are opportunities for using improved grasses and for improved range management, but these are limited and slow to be realized.

Another potentially serious constraint on efforts to expand supplies of high-quality protein is the inability of scientists to achieve a breakthrough in per acre yields of soybeans. Soybeans are consumed directly as food by more than a billion people throughout densely populated East Asia, and they are an important high-quality protein ingredient in livestock and poultry feeds throughout the world. The importance of soybeans in the world food economy is indicated by the fact that they have become the leading export product of the United States—surpassing export sales of wheat, corn, and such high-technology items as electronic computers and jet aircraft.

In the United States, which now produces two-thirds of the world's soybean crop and supplies more than four-fifths of all soybeans entering the world market, soybean yields per acre have increased by just over 1 percent per year since 1950; corn yields, on the other hand, have increased by nearly 4 percent per year. One reason soybean yields have not climbed very rapidly is that the soybean, a legume with a built-in nitrogen supply, is not very responsive to nitrogen fertilizer.

In these circumstances, more soybeans are produced essentially by planting more land to soybeans. Almost 85 percent of the dramatic fourfold increase in the U.S. soybean crop since 1950 has come from expanding the area devoted to it. As long as there was ample idle cropland available, this did not pose a problem, but with this cropland reserve rapidly disappearing and with one in every six acres of U.S. cropland already planted to soybeans by 1973, serious supply problems could emerge.

Deep Trouble in Ocean Fisheries

The oceans are one of mankind's major sources of protein. From 1950 to 1970, the world fish catch expanded rapidly, going from 21 million to 70 million tons. This phenomenal growth in the catch of nearly 5 percent, which far exceeded the annual rate of world population growth, greatly increased the average supply of marine protein per person.

But since 1970, the catch has declined for three consecutive years, falling by an estimated 8 million tons (see Table 6). With population continuing to grow, the per capita availability of fish declined 16

Table 6. World Fish Catch: Total and Per Capita

YEAR	TOTAL CATCH	PER CAPITA
	(million metric tons)	(kilograms)
1950	21	8
1951	24	10
1952	25	10
1953	25	10
1954	28	10
1955	29	11
1956	30	11
1957	32	11
1958	33	12
1959	36	13
1960	40	14
1961	43	14
1962	46	15
1963	48	15
1964	52	16
1965	52	16
1966	57	17
1967	60	18
1968	63	18
1969	63	18
1970	70	19
1971	69	19
1972 (prel.)	64	17
1973 (prel.)	62	16

SOURCE: 1950–71 data from FAO, *Yearbook of Fisheries Statistics,* various issues. Data for 1972 and 1973 are author estimates based on preliminary FAO data.

percent during this three-year span, triggering dramatic price rises. As stocks of many key commercial species are depleted, the amount of time and capital expended to bring in the shrinking catch continues to rise every year.

Many marine biologists now feel that the global catch of table-grade fish is at or near the maximum sustainable level. A large number of the thirty or so leading species of commercial-grade fish currently may be overfished; that is, stocks will not sustain even the current catch.

If the world fish catch stabilizes or declines, then that share of the growing global demand for protein until recently filled by growth in the fish catch must now either be filled by a stepped-up expansion of land-based protein supplies or be choked off by further price rises.

There is no prospect for the foreseeable future that the expansion of fish farming could amount to more than a small fraction of the former annual growth in the ocean fish catch, which until recently increased by 2 to 3 million tons yearly. Any substantial contribution to growth in the global fish supply from fish farming awaits further advances in technology and extensive capital investment in fish farming facilities.

World fishery resources are an important source of protein. The catch in recent years has amounted to nearly 40 pounds (live weight) per person. Of this catch roughly 60 percent was table-grade fish, the remainder consisting of species used for manufacturing fish meal, which in turn is used in poultry and hog feed in the industrial countries. In two of the world's more populous nations, Japan and the Soviet Union, fish are very significant as a direct source of protein in the national diet. Direct fish consumption per person in Japan totals 70 pounds per year, the highest of any major country.

In sum, despite the substantial opportunities for expanding the world's food output, it now seems likely that the supply of food, particularly protein, will lag behind the growth in demand for some time to come, resulting in significantly higher prices during the decade ahead than those of the 1960s. We are witnessing the transformation of the world protein market from a buyer's to a seller's market, much as the world energy market has been transformed over the past few years.

Scarce Resources: Land, Water, and Energy

As the world demand for food climbs, constraints on efforts to expand food production become increasingly apparent. The means of expanding food supplies from conventional agriculture fall into two categories: either increasing the amount of land under cultivation, or raising yields on existing cropland through intensified use of water, energy, and fertilizers. In either direction, we face scarcity problems.

From the beginning of agriculture until about 1950, expanding the cultivated area was the major means of increasing the world's food supply. Since mid-century, however, raising output on existing cultivated area has accounted for most of the increase. Intensification of cultivation has progressed steadily since 1950; during the early 1970s it has accounted for an estimated four-fifths of the annual growth in world food output, far overshadowing expansion of the cultivated area.

The traditional approach to increasing production—extending the area under cultivation—has only limited scope for the future. Indeed, some parts of the world face a net reduction in agricultural land because of the growth in competing uses, such as recreation, transportation, and industrial and residential development. Few countries have well-defined land use policies that protect agricultural land from other uses. In the United States, vast areas of farmland have been diverted indiscriminately to other purposes in recent years, with little thought to the possible long-term consequences.

Some more densely populated countries, such as Japan and several Western European countries, have been experiencing a reduction in the land used for crop production for several decades. Other parts of the world, including particularly the Indian subcontinent, the Middle East, North and sub-Saharan Africa, the Caribbean, Central America, and the Andean countries, are losing disturbingly large acreages of cropland each year because of severe soil erosion.

The availability of arable land is important, but perhaps even more important for the future will be the availability of water for agricultural purposes. In many regions of the world, fertile agricultural land is available if water can be found to make it produce. Yet most of the rivers that lend themselves to damming and to irrigation have already been developed. During the third quarter of this century, the expansion of the world's irrigated acreage has been dramatic but, as we run out of easy opportunities to construct new irrigation reservoirs, the growth in irrigation is slowing markedly. Future efforts to expand fresh water supplies for agricultural purposes will increasingly focus on such techniques as the diversion of rivers (as in the Soviet Union), the manipulation of rainfall patterns to increase the share of rain falling over moisture-deficient agricultural areas, and eventually, depending on the cost of energy, the desalting of sea water.

The intensification of agricultural production on existing cultivated area in most developing countries will involve a severalfold increase in energy requirements. Energy is required for more thorough seedbed preparation, weeding, irrigation pumps, application of fertilizer and pesticides, and for harvesting the heavier crop. With world energy prices rising rapidly, the costs of intensifying food production will rise commensurately. In countries already engaged in high-energy agriculture, such as the United States, Japan, and those in Western Europe, high energy prices may reduce future food production prospects below what they would otherwise be.

The future availability of fertilizer will be directly affected by the scarcity of energy. Manufacture of nitrogen fertilizer, the most widely used chemical fertilizer, commonly utilizes natural gas or naphtha as a raw material, and the manufacturing process itself consumes large amounts of energy. Fertilizer is already in short supply, largely because of a lag in the construction of new production facilities, but the high cost of energy inputs will also ensure higher fertilizer prices. Yet fertilizer requirements over the remaining years of this century will soar to phenomenal levels.

Even more ominous than the price rises are the absolute shortages of fertilizers which appeared in 1973. By early 1974, there were signs that many nations—including some very populous ones, such as Indonesia, India, and the Philippines—would be unable to obtain the needed amounts of fertilizer *regardless of price*. Japan, a principal supplier of nitrogenous fertilizers in Asia, was forced to cut production and exports substantially as a result of the energy crisis. Simultaneously, the United States, due to the combination of increased fertilizer demand accompanying the return of idle land to production and energy shortages, reduced its fertilizer exports. In early 1974, it appeared virtually certain that reduced fertilizer supplies would cause a drop in food production in the 1974–75 crop year in several key developing countries even with favorable weather conditions. The only real question was how large the fall in production would be. Food import needs of these nations will be increased at a time when global reserves are already at dangerously low levels and food prices are at historic highs.

One of the key questions concerning future gains in agricultural production is whether the more advanced countries can sustain the trend of rising per acre yields of cereals. In some countries, the rate of increase in per acre yields for certain crops is beginning to slow, and the capital investments required for each additional increase may now start to climb sharply. In agriculturally advanced countries such as Japan, and some in Europe, the cost of further raising the yield per acre for some crops is already rising. For example, raising rice yields in Japan from the current 5,000 pounds per acre to 6,000 pounds would be very costly. Raising yields of corn in the United States from 90 to 100 bushels per acre is requiring a much larger quantity of nitrogen than was needed to raise yields from 50 to 60 bushels. Higher fertilizer prices will, in this context, further reduce the potential for continuing yield increases.

The Green Revolution: Opportunity Lost?

Efforts to modernize agriculture in the poor countries in the 1950s and early 1960s were well-intentioned but frequently frustrated. When farmers in these countries attempted to use varieties of corn developed for Iowa, they often failed to produce any corn at all. Japanese rice varieties introduced into India were not suited to either local cultural practices or consumer tastes. Intensive application of fertilizer to local cereal varieties often resulted in a limited, and occasionally even negative, yield response.

It was against this backdrop of frustration that a Rockefeller Foundation team under the leadership of Nobel Prize winner Dr. Norman Borlaug developed the high-yield dwarf wheats in Mexico in the 1950s. Three unique characteristics of these wheats endeared them to farmers in many countries—their fertilizer responsiveness, lack of photoperiod (day length) sensitivity, and early maturity.

When farmers applied more than 40 pounds of nitrogen fertilizer per acre to traditional varieties having tall, thin straw, the wheat often lodged or fell over, causing severe crop losses. By contrast, nitrogen applications to the short, stiff-strawed dwarf varieties of Mexican wheat allowed the efficient application of up to 120 pounds of nutrient per acre. Given the necessary fertilizer and water and the appropriate management, farmers found they could easily double the yields they had been getting from indigenous varieties.

Beyond this, the reduced sensitivity of dwarf varieties to day length permitted them to be moved around the world over a wide range of latitudes, stretching from Mexico, which lies partly in the tropics, to Turkey in the temperate zone. Because the biological clocks of the new wheats were much less sensitive than those of the traditional ones, planting dates were much more flexible. Another advantageous characteristic of the new wheats was their early maturity. They were ready for harvest within 120 days after planting; the traditional varieties took 150 days or more. This trait, combined with the reduced sensitivity to day length, created broad new opportunities for multiple cropping (the harvesting of more than one crop per year on the same land) wherever water supplies were sufficient.

Within a few years after the spectacular breakthrough with wheat in Mexico, the Ford Foundation joined the Rockefeller Foundation to establish the International Rice Research Institute (IRRI) in the Philippines. Its purpose was to attempt to breed a fertilizer-responsive, early-maturing rice capable of wide adaptation—in effect, a counterpart of the high-yield wheats. With the wheat experience to draw upon, agricultural scientists at IRRI struck pay dirt quickly. Within a few years, they released the first of the high-yield dwarf rices, a variety known as IR-8.

The great advantage of the new seeds was that they permitted developing countries to utilize quickly agricultural research that had taken decades to complete in the United States, Japan, and elsewhere. In those areas of the developing countries where there were requisite supplies of water and fertilizer, and appropriate price incentives were offered, the spread of the high-yield varieties of wheat and rice was rapid. Farmers assumed to be bound by tradition were quick to adopt the new seeds when it was obviously profitable for them to do so.

Early in 1968, the term "Green Revolution" was coined to describe the introduction and rapid spread of the high-yield wheats and rices. In 1965, land planted with these new varieties in Asia totaled about 200 acres, largely trial and demonstration plots. Thereafter, according to figures compiled by Dana Dalrymple of the U.S. Department of Agriculture, the acreage spread swiftly, as follows:

YEAR	ACRES
1965	200
1966	41,000
1967	4,047,000
1968	16,660,000
1969	31,319,000
1970	43,914,000
1971	50,549,000
1972	68,200,000
1973 (prel.)	80,800,000

Acreage figures for Mexico are not included in the series above, since the new wheat had largely displaced traditional varieties before the Green Revolution became an international phenomenon in the mid-1960s. Among the principal Asian countries to benefit from using the new seeds are India, Pakistan, Turkey, the Philippines, and, more recently, Malaysia, Indonesia, and Sri Lanka.

During the late 1960s, the Philippines was able to achieve self-sufficiency in rice, ending a half century of dependence on imports. Unfortunately, this situation was not sustained because of a variety of factors, including civil unrest, the susceptibility of the new rices to disease, and the failure of the government to continue the essential support of the rice program.

Pakistan greatly increased its wheat production, emerging as a net exporter of grain in recent years. In India, where advances in the new varieties were concentrated largely in wheat, progress has been encouraging. During the seven-year span from 1965 to 1972, India expanded its wheat production from 11 million tons to 27 million tons, an increase in a major crop unmatched by any other country in history.

One result of this dramatic advance in wheat production in India was the accumulation of unprecedented cereal reserves and the attainment of temporary cereal self-sufficiency in 1972. This eliminated, at least temporarily, the need for imports into a country that only a few years before had been the principal recipient of U.S. food aid. Economic self-sufficiency in cereals—when farmers produce as much as consumers can afford at prevailing prices—is not to be confused with nutritional self-sufficiency, however, which requires much higher levels of productivity and purchasing power.

During late 1971 and in 1972, India was able to use nearly 2 million tons from its own food reserves, initially to feed nearly 10 million Bengali refugees during the civil war in East Pakistan, and later as food aid for newly independent Bangladesh. A poor monsoon in 1972 forced India back into the world market as an importer of grain, but on a much smaller scale—4 million tons—than the massive import of nearly 10 million tons that followed the 1965 monsoon failure.

This is not to suggest that the Green Revolution has, by any stretch of the imagination, solved the world's food problems, either on a short- or long-term basis. The 1972 drought clearly demonstrated that Indian agriculture is still at the mercy of the weather. A second monsoon failure would seriously disrupt the pattern of progress that has characterized Indian agriculture over the past five years. The fertilizer shortage emerging in 1974, impairing the effectiveness of the high-yield cereals, will probably contribute to rapid growth in the need for Indian food imports, though the potential magnitude was not yet clear by early 1974.

It has been fashionable in many circles to criticize the Green Revolution, but it can be properly assessed only when we ask what things would have been like in its absence. The alternative scenario is a grim one and helps put its accomplishments in appropriate perspective. Increases in cereal production made possible by the new seeds did arrest the deteriorating trend in per capita food production of the early 1960s in the developing countries. The massive famine anticipated by many has been thus far avoided. Although relatively little progress has been made in raising the per capita production of cereals among the poor countries as a whole, it brought spectacular localized successes in raising cereal output. In sum, the Green Revolution does not represent a solution to the food problem; rather, it has been a means of buying time, perhaps an additional fifteen years, during which some way might be found to apply the brakes to population growth.

Almost a decade has now passed since the launching of the Green Revolution, but success stories in national family planning programs in the poor nations are too few. Among the population giants of Asia, China appears to be substantially reducing its birth rate and India is very gradually bringing its birth rate down, but reductions to date in Indonesia, Pakistan, and Bangladesh are minimal. The futility of relying solely on the new agricultural technologies to "solve" the population problem is evident in Mexico, the country where the Green Revolution began. Fifteen years of dramatic advances in wheat production made Mexico a net exporter of cereals in the late 1960s, but a population growth rate that ranks among the highest in the world has again converted Mexico into an importer of food.

Growing Global Food Insecurity

The period since World War II has been characterized by chronic excess capacity in world agriculture, much of it concentrated in the United States. The world had, in effect, two major food reserves during this period. One was in the form of actual grain reserves in the principal exporting countries and the other in the form of roughly 50 million acres of idle cropland, virtually all of it land held out of production under farm subsidy programs in the United States. Though not as quickly available as the grain reserves, most of this acreage has been brought back into production within 12 to 18 months once the decision was made to do so.

Grain reserves, including both food grains and feed grains, are most commonly measured in terms of carry-over stocks—the amount in storage at the time the new crop begins to come in. World carry-over stocks have traditionally been concentrated in a few of the principal exporting countries—the United States, Canada, Australia, and Argentina. Since 1960, world grain reserves have fluctuated from a high of 155 million metric tons to a low of about 100 million metric tons. When these reserves drop near 100 million tons, severe shortages and strong upward price pressures develop. Although 100 million tons appears to be an enormous quantity of grain, it represents a mere 8 percent of annual world grain consumption—an uncomfortably small working reserve. As world consumption expands by some 2.5 percent annually, so should the size of working reserves; instead reserves have dwindled over the past two decades while consumption has continued to climb. Reserves totaled only 105 million tons in 1973 and are expected to fall lower in 1974.

The need to utilize the reserve of idle cropland has also occurred with increasing frequency in recent years. This first happened during the food crisis years of 1966 and 1967, when world grain reserves were reduced to a dangerously low level and the United States temporarily brought back into production a small portion of the 50 million idle acres. It was dipped into again in 1971, as a result of a corn blight threat in the United States. In 1973, when world grain reserves once more declined in response to the growing scarcity of food in relation to demand, the United States again resorted to cultivating its idle cropland, but to a much greater degree than on either of the two previous occasions. Government decisions in early 1973 permitted most of the acreage to come back into production, with the remainder released for production in 1974.

By combining global reserve stocks of grain with the grain production potential of idle cropland, we may obtain a good indication of the total reserve capacity in the world food economy in any given year. As a percentage of total world grain consumption in any given year, this total provides a rough quantitative indicator of global food security. As Figure 2 and Table 7 demonstrate, the world is now in an extremely vulnerable position. In 1974, world reserve capabilities in relation to consumption needs have fallen far lower than at any time during the past quarter century. Reserves have dwindled from the equivalent of 95 days of world grain consumption in 1961 to only 27 days in 1974, a fragile buffer against the vagaries of weather or plant disease.

From the end of World War II until quite recently, world prices for the principal temperate zone farm commodities, such as wheat, feed grains, and soybeans, have been remarkably stable. In part, this is because world prices throughout much of this period have rested on the commodity support level in the United States. Since world food stocks may remain chronically low and there may not be any idle cropland in the United States, there is a very real prospect of exceedingly volatile world prices for principal food commodities.

Redefining Famine

High food prices and shortages are an inconvenience for the more affluent societies and individuals, but the poor nations, and the poor within nations, are in a genuinely dangerous predicament. High prices may not only keep needed food out of the reach of poor nations and individuals, but when global reserve stocks are low, the capacity of the international community to respond with food aid in emergencies such as droughts or crop failures is greatly diminished.

When one spends about 80 percent of one's income on food, as does a sizable segment of mankind, a doubling in the price of wheat or rice cannot possibly be offset by increased expenditures. It can only drive a subsistence diet below the survival level. One reason it is possible for the world's affluent to ignore such tragedies is that changes have occurred in the way that famine manifests itself. In earlier historical periods, famine was largely a geographic phenomenon. Whole nations

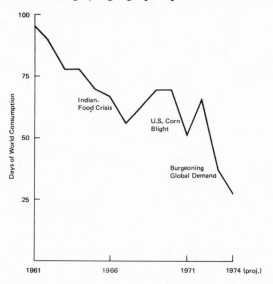

Figure 2
World Grain Reserves as Days of World Consumption
(Includes Production Potential of Idled U.S. Cropland)

Source: Based on U.S. Dept. of Agriculture Data.

Table 7. *Index of World Food Security*

YEAR	RESERVE STOCKS OF GRAIN	GRAIN EQUIVALENT OF IDLE U.S. CROPLAND	TOTAL RESERVES	RESERVES AS DAYS OF ANNUAL WORLD GRAIN CONSUMPTION
	(million metric tons)			(days)
1961	154	68	222	95
1962	131	81	212	88
1963	125	70	195	77
1964	128	70	198	77
1965	113	71	184	69
1966	99	79	178	66
1967	100	51	151	55
1968	116	61	177	62
1969	136	73	209	69
1970	146	71	217	69
1971	120	41	161	51
1972	131	78	209	66
1973	103	20	123	37
1974 (proj.)	89	0	89	27

SOURCE: Derived from U.S. Department of Agriculture data.

or regions, whether Ireland in 1847 or West Bengal in 1943, experienced widespread starvation and death. Today the advancements in both national and international distribution systems have concentrated the effects of food scarcity among the world's poor, wherever they are. The modern version of famine does not lend itself so readily to dramatic photographs, such as those of the morning ritual of collecting bodies in Calcutta during the Bengal famine of 1943, but it is no less real in the human toll it exacts.

As prices are driven up, seriously limiting the ability of many less developed countries (and particularly of the poor within those countries) to buy needed food, sources of food aid dry up as well. Since the American food aid program under Public Law 480 is largely predicated upon the existence of surpluses, this program is cut severely in time of scarcity. In fiscal year 1974, shipments of wheat are

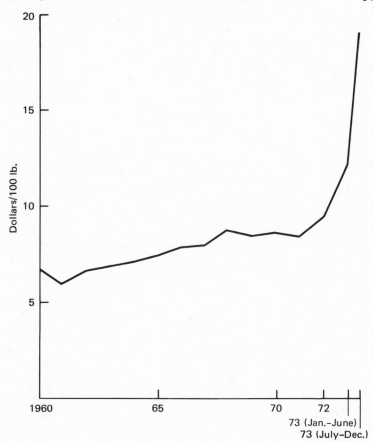

Figure 3
World Rice Price, 1960–1973
(Unit Value of U.S. Exports)

Source: U.S. Dept. of Agriculture

less than one-third those of two years before, rice, feed grains, and vegetable oils are less than half, and shipments of milk have ceased entirely.

Many private and governmental humanitarian programs in the developing nations are heavily dependent upon food grants from the United States. Concessional sales of food to poor nations have

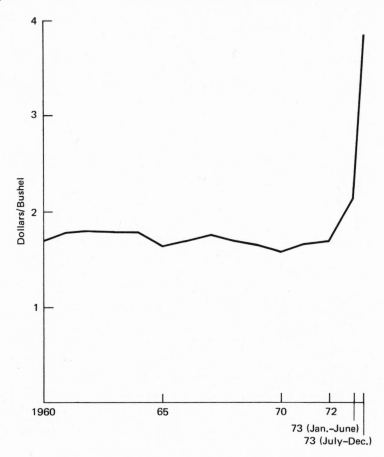

Figure 4
World Wheat Price, 1960–1973
(Unit Value of U.S. Exports)

Source: U.S. Dept. of Agriculture

sometimes proved to be a powerful boost to local economic development efforts, and disaster relief shipments have helped avert large-scale famine on many occasions, most recently in sub-Saharan Africa.

With the prospect of chronic global food scarcity for the foreseeable future, the United States must undertake a major and conscientious

Table 8. *World Prices of Major Food Commodities, 1960–73*
(unit value of U.S. exports)

	RICE (dollars/ 100 lbs.)	WHEAT (dollars/ bushel)	SOYBEANS (dollars/ bushel)
1960	$6.62	$1.69	$2.27
1961	5.99	1.77	2.41
1962	6.62	1.81	2.41
1963	6.77	1.79	2.58
1964	7.02	1.80	2.71
1965	7.21	1.63	2.85
1966	7.79	1.69	3.09
1967	7.80	1.74	2.93
1968	8.61	1.68	2.75
1969	8.44	1.64	2.64
1970	8.48	1.58	2.79
1971	8.41	1.68	3.13
1972	9.40	1.75	3.38
1973 (Jan.–June)	12.00	2.12	5.35
1973 (July–Dec.) (prel.)	19.00	3.80	6.20

SOURCE: IMF, *International Financial Statistics* and U.S. Department of Agriculture.

reassessment of its food aid program. As the only nation with the capacity unilaterally to carry on a sizable food aid program, the United States must recognize a rationale for food aid which goes beyond the mere disposal of costly domestic surplus stocks. New legislation is needed to ensure the availability of needed levels of grant and concessionary food aid to poor countries *whether or not commercial surpluses exist at the time.* If the United States would decide to channel a greater share of future food aid through a multilateral arrangement such as the World Food Programme of the FAO, then other economically advanced nations which do not have bilateral food aid programs might be willing to do more.

Agronomic Potential of the Poor Countries

Over the longer run, the world's greatest reservoir of unexploited food potential appears to be in the less developed countries. In those countries having the appropriate economic incentives, fertilizer, water, and other required agricultural inputs and supporting institutions, the introduction of new wheat and rice varieties has increased production substantially. But the recent jump in per acre yields in many developing countries appears so dramatic largely because their yields traditionally have been so low relative to the potential. Today rice yields per acre in India and Nigeria still average only one-third those of Japan; corn yields in Thailand and Brazil are less than one-third those of the United States. Large increases in food supply are possible in these countries with a much smaller increment of resources than in agriculturally advanced nations if farmers are given the necessary economic incentives, are provided with supporting services such as credit and technical services, and have access to the requisite inputs.

Since most farmers in less developed nations are using very little fertilizer per acre, additional fertilizer applications in these nations would bring much higher yield gains than comparable additional fertilizer applications in the agriculturally advanced nations. Ironically, as fertilizer scarcity develops, the developed nations are reducing sales to the poorer nations, where the additional food produced per ton of fertilizer is far greater.

India and the United States have about the same crop area, with somewhat similar characteristics. If Indian yield levels equaled those of the United States, India's current annual cereal production would be 230 million metric tons rather than the present total of nearly 100 million tons. If rice farmers in Bangladesh attained Japanese yield levels, rice production would jump more than threefold, rising from 12 to 39 million tons. Brazil, by doubling its present cultivated area, could produce an additional 22 million tons of grain even if its currently low yield levels were not improved.

At a point in history when global food scarcity exists and the capacity of the international community to respond to food emergencies has diminished, a convincing case can be made for strengthened support of agricultural development in such populous food-short countries as Bangladesh, India, Indonesia, and Nigeria. An almost equally convincing case can be made for giving particular attention to effectively involving small farmers in the production effort. There is evidence that small farmers, when they have effective access to agricultural inputs as well as health and education services, engage in labor intensive agriculture and generally average considerably higher yields per acre than do farmers on large holdings using hired labor or tractors.

Concentrating international assistance efforts on the expansion of food production in the poor countries could reduce upward pressure on world food prices, create additional employment in countries where continuously rising unemployment poses a serious threat to political stability, raise income, and improve nutrition for the poorest portion of humanity. Because this would help satisfy basic social needs, it would also help create the motivation for smaller families, which is a prerequisite to a substantial reduction in birth rates.

5

Population Growth and Environmental Stress

There are numerous environmental costs and stresses associated with continuing population growth and rising affluence in a finite global ecosystem. No effort will be made here to separate the effect of the two, but it is recognized that both contribute, to a greater or lesser degree, to each of the environmental stresses discussed. Among the more disturbing are the rising incidence of environmentally induced illnesses, the lengthening list of endangered species, the growing incidence of inadvertent climate modification, progressive eutrophication of lakes and streams, and ecological undermining of the world food economy.

Environmentally Induced Illnesses

Environmentally induced illnesses result from both the introduction of toxic materials into our environment and the creation of conditions conducive to the rapid spread of certain infectious diseases. Air pollution, a problem in every major city of the world, has reached serious levels in some cities. Los Angeles schoolchildren are cautioned against vigorous play because of air pollution. Tokyo traffic policemen inhale pure oxygen from oxygen tanks every two hours to avoid carbon monoxide poisoning. Medical studies have demonstrated a strong relationship between the level of air pollution and the incidence of respiratory diseases, particularly bronchitis, emphysema, and lung cancer. In the United Kingdom, deaths due to bronchitis are twice as frequent in urban areas with heavily polluted air as in rural areas. A study in the United States based on data from 46 states shows deaths due to lung cancer among lifelong urban residents to be double those of lifelong rural residents. A similar situation exists in England and Wales. The incidence of emphysema in the United States is now increasing rapidly, doubling every seven years. Closely associated with rising levels of air pollution, it is reaching almost epidemic proportions in some cities. Post-mortem respiratory examinations of a group of 45-year-old men in St. Louis revealed evidence of emphysema in nearly half of them.

There is also disturbing evidence of the relationship between air pollution and both stomach cancer and coronary disease. This alarming contribution of air pollution to the incidence of disease and death may at least partly explain why life expectancy among American males did not increase during the 1960s despite impressive advances in medical technology and a vast rise in health service expenditures.

Another source of concern is the rapidly rising level of toxic compounds now circulating in the biosphere, including mercury, lead, arsenic, and cadmium. Forms of life as we know them today, including man, evolved in an environment with very low concentrations of mercury, lead, and cadmium. No one really knows what the long-term consequences will be of increasing the amount of these persistent compounds in circulation in the ecosystem through the continued mining of subterranean deposits. Concentrations have reached a point in some localities where they adversely affect human well-being, causing not only discomfort but sickness and death. One fact that is known is that when the mercury content in water, fish, and other foods reaches a certain level, the central nervous system of more complex organisms, particularly man, begin to be affected. Known deaths from mercury poisoning have occurred in such widely situated areas as Japan (89 deaths), West Pakistan (4), Iraq (300), and Guatemala (20). In Japan, 22 brain-damaged children were born to mothers who did not have enough mercury in their bodies to exhibit symptoms of mercury poisoning, but did have enough to affect the especially vulnerable fetus.

The mercury content of 89 percent of the swordfish on sale in markets in the United States in 1971 was above the tolerance level established by the Food and Drug Administration, causing the agency to advise against further swordfish consumption by Americans. For similar reasons, the government of Sweden recommends that Swedes limit fish consumption to one serving per week. The Japanese Ministry of Health has urged the Japanese people to restrict their intake of fish, traditionally a staple of the Japanese diet.

Effects of lead on health are reported with mounting frequency as a result of the enormous quantities of lead now introduced into the biological system each year. An estimated 500 million additional pounds from our underground reserves were discharged into the environment in the United States alone in 1970. Most lead absorbed by individuals comes from automobile exhaust fumes, plumbing systems, and lead-based paint. New York City reported 2,600 cases of lead poisoning in 1970. Health officials in Washington, D.C., estimate that 5,000 children in that city have more lead in their blood than is safe, and 500 are so seriously affected that they should be hospitalized immediately. A large proportion of the children living in urban areas in the United Kingdom, where the lead content of the air is 20 times that in the countryside, may have higher blood levels of lead than is safe.

Other waste metals such as arsenic, cadmium, and selenium have reached the point where concentrations are adversely affecting human health. A Japanese court ruled in 1971 on behalf of 400 victims of cadmium poisoning who sued an industrial firm for damages. Farmers in the Chofu municipal region near Tokyo were not permitted to market their 1970 spinach crop because its cadmium content exceeded safety levels. Cadmium poses a particularly serious threat because it persists in the human body for decades after it is absorbed.

The growing presence of asbestos fibers in the air and water of industrial countries is generating deep concern among health authorities. Valued for its tough, fire-resistant qualities, asbestos is used in a variety of modern products including building insulation, petrochemicals, fireproof clothing, talcum powder, and brake linings. Asbestiosis, a lung disease that causes breathing difficulties and often eventual death by suffocation or heart attack, has long been known to affect a significant portion of workers in industries utilizing asbestos, and others who are exposed to asbestos dust in high concentrations.

Even more ominous has been the discovery that the inhalation of high concentrations of asbestos fibers greatly increases the chances of death from lung cancer, and from a cancer of the chest or abdomen lining known as mesothelioma. Recent evidence has also linked exposure to asbestos with cancers of the stomach, colon, and rectum. The role of asbestos in causing cancer has received widespread attention only in the last decade. In part, this is because the fatal symptoms of asbestos-induced cancer often do not appear until 25 to 30 years after the exposure. Thus the expanded use of asbestos during World War II, particularly in shipbuilding, has only recently begun taking its toll as former workers fall prey to lung cancer or mesothelioma.

While those who must work with asbestos and those who are directly exposed to high levels of asbestos pollution are in the most obvious danger, investigators report that asbestos in at least trace amounts has become ubiquitous in many industrial societies—appearing in the air, water, food, and beverages. One leading medical authority, Dr. Irving Selikoff, reports that residents of the United States are "all contaminated with asbestos." The possible effects of this trend are not known; what is known, however, is that once asbestos particles are embedded in the lungs, they remain there.

Wherever man has descended into the earth to extract coal, he has been plagued by the life-shortening, debilitating respiratory ailment pneumoconiosis, more commonly known as black lung disease. The daily inhalation and accumulation of coal dust in miners' lungs impairs their ability to absorb oxygen from the air, resulting in extreme shortness of breath and an often fatal vulnerability to other respiratory ailments and heart failure.

Only in the twentieth century has black lung disease been openly recognized by the world medical community and, in some cases, confronted by governments or mining industries. In much of Europe and in Australia it has been nearly eliminated over the last generation through investment in new dust-catching technologies in mines. In the United States progress has been slower, and by the early 1970s some 30 percent of American mines had not yet met federal dust control standards. Coal industry spokesmen claimed to be spending an additional $1 billion on required health and safety improvements. Since 1969, the United States government has accepted responsibility for the welfare of black lung victims, paying in 1972 over $500 million to 255,000 stricken miners—or their widows. Government statisticians estimate a cumulative expenditure of $8.4 billion in compensation by the time the existing program expires in 1981. Even with reimbursement, the quarter of a million victims of this debilitating disease have paid an incalculably high price to provide cheap energy for the rest of society.

Throughout the tropical, poorer countries, an even greater threat to human well-being is the snail-borne disease schistosomiasis, or bilharzia. Now that malaria has been eradicated in many areas, schistosomiasis is the world's leading infectious disease, affecting some 200 million people in North Africa, the Middle East, sub-Saharan Africa, South Asia, East Asia, the Caribbean, and the northeast coast of Latin America. Though seldom immediately fatal, it inflicts upon its victims a debilitated existence with a recurrent fever and diarrhea.

Labeled by some the "poor man's emphysema," schistosomiasis is a persistent disease that thrives in areas under continuous irrigation.

The disease has spread rapidly in the developing world, where the expansion of irrigation systems has created an ideal environment for the alternate host of the parasites, a fresh-water snail. It is most often contracted by barefoot workers in flooded rice fields, whose skin is penetrated by the aquatic parasite. The schistosomes, or tiny worms, then migrate through the bloodstream and lodge themselves in the liver, where they reproduce. The eggs are excreted with body wastes, often ending up in irrigation canals, open sewers, and drainage ditches. Here they are hatched and are once again taken up by the snail, thus completing their life cycle. The disease is most prevalent in areas where human excrement is used as fertilizer, such as China, and where there is frequent flooding or where a common lagoon serves as a common source of community water for everything from washing clothes to bathing.

As of 1974, the share of the world's population suffering from environmentally induced diseases appears to be increasing steadily, numbering in the hundreds of millions. These victims of mass alterations in the environment are bearing a disproportionately large share of the costs of the continually expanding economic activity and human numbers.

Endangered Species

Man is not the only species threatened by the deteriorating natural environment. Indeed, many animals have a much lower tolerance than man. Thus far during this century, an average of one species per year quietly made its exit somewhere in the world. As the number of human beings goes up, the number of extant species goes down. The Department of the Interior's list of endangered species of mammals, birds, and fish within the United States now totals more than a hundred. One recent worldwide list of endangered animal species, though obviously far from complete, includes 982 mammals, birds, reptiles, amphibians, and fish. As we move upward along the steeply inclined curve of population growth, new species are added to the list almost weekly.

Numerous species of Asia's mammals, most notably the Bengal tiger and the Indian rhinoceros, are being endangered by the explosive increase in the human population. Recent reports indicate that fewer than 20 clouded leopards remain in Bangladesh's Chittagong hill tracts. Fewer than 4,000 of man's close kin, the orangutan, remain in Indonesia. Today there are no more than 2,500 wild elephants in Sri Lanka, fewer than half the number twenty years ago. Their source of subsistence is diminishing steadily as their forest and jungle habitat is cleared to produce food for the island's population, now doubling every 32 years.

Pravda reports that the reckless use of chemical pesticides in agriculture is decimating many forms of wildlife in the Soviet Union, causing many species to become "zoological rarities." The duckhunting season was reportedly canceled in 1970 because of the declining number of ducks. According to *Pravda,* now beginning to sound increasingly like Rachel Carson, "This question [the extinction of species] is worrying us more and more every year. Why do we see almost no flocks of geese and cranes in April? Almost all the partridges are gone. Our woods, gardens, and fields are becoming quieter and quieter." In Denmark, the return of the storks from wintering in North Africa has long been a national event celebrated by young and old alike. At one time, 10,000 storks arrived each year; in 1973, only 70 pairs came. The use of pesticides by farmers to control the locust in East Africa and the Nile River valley is apparently eliminating the storks as well. In the United States, the bald eagle, the national symbol, is now threatened with extinction by an intolerable level in the biosphere of non-biodegradable pesticides, particularly dieldrin.

Swedish zoologist Kai Curry-Lindahl estimates that more than 300 species and subspecies of animals have already vanished from the face of the earth as a result of man's activities. Once destroyed, these species cannot be re-created by man, however sophisticated modern technology might be. This trend can be reversed only by cooperation on a global scale. Failure to achieve the needed degree of cooperation will mean that, in this area at least, the demands on the natural system generated by man have become unmanageable, causing an irreversible decline in the quality of human life. The great difficulty here is attaching a price tag to the extinction of some species of wildlife. Since the extinct species is lost forever, any value at all, if calculated to infinity, would necessarily exceed any short-term gain from the activities causing the extinction.

Inadvertent Climate Modification

Efforts to meet mankind's expanding needs for food, energy, and material goods are creating seemingly endless possibilities for altering the earth's climate either intentionally or unintentionally. The list of ways in which man may be inadvertently affecting the earth's climate, at least locally, is a long one. The list includes the consumption of energy—which can either warm local areas, as in urban heat centers which are measurably warmer than surrounding areas, or contribute to a cooling of the earth by discharging dust particles into the atmosphere and thus reducing the inflow of solar energy. Agricultural activity, especially bringing marginal land under the plow, can result in dust-bowl conditions, with similar effects on the flow of solar energy.

Climatological data show that the earth's average temperature rose about 0.4 degree centigrade or one degree Fahrenheit between 1880 and 1940. Since 1940, however, it has dropped 0.5 degree Fahrenheit. No one can say whether this observed temperature decline in the past twenty-five years was due to long-term natural cyclical changes, to increased particulate matter in the upper atmosphere from volcanic activity, to the expansion of agricultural dust bowls in parts of Africa and Asia, to expanding industrial activity, or to some factor not yet observed. What is significant is that climatologists do agree that man's activities are now at a scale which can affect, and may already be affecting, the earth's climate.

What is not clear is the specific and relative climatic effect of various activities. Some tend to warm the earth, others to cool it. The precise net effect remains a mystery. A report prepared for the United Nations in the summer of 1971 summed up the state of knowledge on the subject: "There can be little doubt that man in the process of reshaping his environment in many ways has changed the climate of large regions of the earth and he has probably had some influences on global climate as well—exactly how much, we do not know."

Eutrophication of Lakes and Streams

One response to the steadily growing demand for food has been the great expansion in the use of chemical fertilizer since mid-century. This expansion has benefited mankind enormously, but the effects have not all been positive. The runoff of chemical fertilizers from farmlands into rivers and lakes is contributing to the eutrophication, or overfertilization, of fresh-water bodies. How much the fertilizer runoff factor is contributing to the eutrophication problem and how much must be attributed to other causes remains an open question. Certainly it varies from situation to situation.

The process itself is clear enough, however. Nitrates and phosphates introduced into fresh water through this runoff process serve as nutrients for algae and other aquatic plant life. Algae particularly thrive and multiply rapidly, resulting in a veritable population explosion. As the vast numbers of algae die and ecompose, the free oxygen supply in lakes and streams is depleted, thus killing off fish life, beginning with those species having the highest oxygen requirements. Apart from its impact on fish and other forms of marine life, the decomposition of the massive population of algae produces foul odors, making water unfit for recreational uses such as swimming or boating. Unarrested eutrophication usually brings about the death of a fresh-water body, converting it into a putrid, smelly swamp.

The growing use of chemical fertilizers is causing another more localized but hazardous problem: the chemical pollution of drinking water. Nitrates are the main worry, since they have risen to toxic levels in some communities in the United States. Both children and livestock have become ill and sometimes died from drinking water that contained high levels of nitrates. Excessive nitrates can cause metahemoglobanemia, a physiological disorder affecting the blood's oxygen-carrying capacity. Since the problem is of local dimensions, it can be effectively countered by finding alternative (though usually more costly) sources of drinking water. Bottled water is being used in some California communities.

Ground-water nitrates in southern Illinois rose above the FDA tolerance levels in the early 1970s, creating enough of a health threat for the state government to hold hearings on the possibility of putting a ceiling on the use of nitrogen fertilizer. Although this possibility was eventually rejected, the limit on application rates that was being considered was below those now used by many Illinois farmers.

Soil Erosion and Abandonment

One consequence of the continuous growth of population and the demand for food is the spread of cultivation onto marginal lands, lands with thin mantles of topsoil that will not sustain continuous and intensive cultivation. Fuel demands for heating and cooking have long exceeded the replacement capacity of local forests, and in many parts of the world the forested area has declined to the point where there is little forest land left. In these circumstances, exemplified by the Indo-Pakistan subcontinent, people are unable to afford fossil fuels and so are reduced to using cow dung for fuel. This expedient, in turn, deprives the soil of badly needed organic matter and nutrients.

Increasing human population in the poor countries is almost always accompanied by a nearly commensurate growth in livestock population. As cattle populations are increased in order to expand draft power and food supplies, they denude the countryside of its natural grass cover. Overgrazing by goats and sheep is even more damaging, affecting trees and shrubs as well. This overgrazing, combined with the progressive deforestation, is resulting in a near total denuding of the countryside in some poor countries, creating conditions for the rapid spread of soil erosion by wind and water. Literally millions of acres of cropland in Asia, the Middle East, Africa, and the Andean countries are being abandoned each year because severe soil erosion has rendered them unproductive or at least incapable of sustaining the local inhabitants with existing agricultural technologies.

It takes centuries to form an inch of topsoil through natural processes, but man is managing to destroy it in some areas of the world in only a fraction of that time. The problems associated with the loss of topsoil do not end with the abandonment of the severely eroded land. Much of the topsoil finds its way into streams and rivers and eventually into irrigation reservoirs and canals. A dramatic and unfortunate example of this indirect loss of soil is provided by the Mangla reservoir recently constructed in the foothills of the Himalayas in West Pakistan. Feasibility studies undertaken in the late 1950s justifying the investment of $600 million in this irrigation project were based on a life expectancy of at least 100 years. As the rapid population growth in the watershed feeding the Mangla reservoir has progressed, so has the rate of denuding and soil erosion. The result is that the reservoir is expected to be completely filled with silt within 50 years.

History provides us with many past examples of man's abuse of the soil that sustains him. North Africa, once the fertile granary of the Roman Empire, is now largely a desert or near desert sustained with food imports. The United States abused its rich agricultural inheritance by overplowing and overgrazing the Great Plains during the early decades of this century, leaving the area vulnerable to the gradually worsening wind erosion that culminated in the dust-bowl era of the 1930s. The United States had the resources, the technical knowhow, and the will to respond to this crisis by the extensive adoption of strip cropping, including the fallowing of 20 million acres, and by constructing literally thousands of windbreaks in the form of rows of trees across the Great Plains. The situation eventually stabilized, and today erosion is negligible in the Great Plains and land productivity is high. Had the United States not been able to respond in this fashion, much of the southern Great Plains, like the once fertile fields of North Africa, would by now have been abandoned.

Many of the world's densely populated regions—such as those in western India, Pakistan, North Africa, and northern China—face similar problems of severe wind and water erosion of their soils because of the acute and growing pressure of human and livestock population on land, but do not have the slack in their food systems to permit the diversion of large acreages to fallow. The rescue of these areas could be achieved by a massive effort involving reforestation of hundreds of millions of acres, the controlled grazing of cattle, terracing, and systematic management of watersheds. But all of these measures require an enormous array of financial resources and technical know-how not now available to the areas that need them most.

The significance of wind erosion goes far beyond the loss of topsoil. As noted earlier, a continuing buildup of particulate matter in the atmosphere, not only from the industrial activities of the rich countries but also from wind erosion of soil in the poorer countries, could affect the earth's climate by reducing the amount of incoming solar energy. Should it be established that an increasing amount of particulate matter in the atmosphere is contributing to the recent cooling trend, the richer countries would have still another reason to provide massive capital and technical assistance to the poor countries, joining with them to confront this common threat to mankind. Clearly, the poorer countries on their own do not have the resources to undertake the necessary effort to arrest and reverse this trend.

Ecological Undermining of the Food Economy

The pressure of the growing demand for food is beginning to undermine local food producing systems in widely separated areas around the world with increasing frequency. Prominent among these are the collapse of the anchovy fishery, the southward movement of the Sahara in Africa, and the devastating flood in Pakistan during August 1973.

One dramatic example of the ultimate effect of excessive pressure on the food producing ecosystem is the current crisis in the anchovy fishery off the western coast of Latin America. Only a few years ago, this vast fishery accounted for one-fifth of the global fish catch. During the late months of 1972, the anchovies seemingly disappeared from the traditional offshore fishing areas. This did not cause a great deal of alarm, since a slight shift in the Humboldt Current and the change in temperature of a few degrees had caused the anchovies to move away temporarily before. But as of early 1974, stocks appear to be seriously depleted. There is now growing evidence that the very heavy offtake from the anchovy fishery, ranging from 10 to 12 million tons in the late 1960s and early 1970s, may have exceeded the capacity of the fishery to regenerate itself. Overfishing may have seriously damaged the anchovy fishery, in effect causing its collapse. No one knows how long it will take for it to recover its full productive capacity. It could be a few years or even a few decades.

A second striking example of visible diminution of the earth's food producing capacity through ecological overstress is now evident in the Sahelian zone south of the Sahara in Africa. For many months in 1973, the news media reported the growing famine situation in the Sahel as simply the product of a sequence of drought years. The problem was presented in terms of the need for a temporary food relief effort, specifically some 600,000 tons of grain to meet a serious food crisis over the next several months in a half-dozen seriously affected countries. This was indeed a problem. The need was real.

Some meteorologists feel that fundamental climatic changes are contributing to the drought situation. But there is also a much more basic problem in the Sahel. Over the past thirty-five years, human and livestock populations along the desert's fringe have increased rapidly, in some areas nearly doubling. As these populations multiply, they put more pressure on the ecosystem than it can withstand. The result is overgrazing, deforestation, and over-all denudation of the land.

This denudation and deforestation has caused the Sahara Desert to begin to move southward at an accelerated rate all along its 3,500-mile southern fringe, stretching from Senegal in the west to northern Ethiopia in the east. A United States government study indicates that the desert is moving southward up to 30 miles per year, depending on where it is measured. As the desert moves southward, human and livestock populations retreat before it. The result is ever greater pressure on the fringe area. This in turn contributes to the denudation and deforestation, setting in process a self-reinforcing cycle.

Coping with this situation requires far more than the temporary panacea of food relief. A relief effort for this region is essential, and will be required for the foreseeable future, but it deals only with symptoms. There is above all a need to attempt to arrest and reverse the southward movement of the desert. This will require a concerted cooperative effort by the tier of countries most immediately affected, by the next tier of countries southward, which will shortly be affected, and by a large number of external donors who must provide an extensive infusion of economic resources and technical know-how in desert reclamation and land management from outside the region. Above all, it calls for a crash effort to slow and stabilize population growth in the region.

The scope of the cooperative effort will have to be comparable to that which launched the Green Revolution in the late 1960s. Anything less will not suffice. Already the second tier of countries below the Sahara is being affected as people and livestock retreat southward and cross national boundaries. If the Sahara continues its southward movement, it will, within a matter of years, begin to encroach upon the second tier of countries as well.

Ecological overstress is today also very much in evidence in the Indian subcontinent. Over the past twenty-five years, as human and livestock populations have expanded, the subcontinent has been progressively deforested. Even several years ago, one did not need much training in soil and water management to predict with alarm the long-term consequences of this accelerating deforestation. It is most serious in the Himalayas and the surrounding foothills, for this is where nearly all the major river systems of the Indian subcontinent —the Indus, the Ganges, and the Brahmaputra—originate.

For anyone who has observed the subcontinent over the past fifteen to twenty years, it should not have come as any surprise to read during the late summer of 1973 of the worst flood in Pakistan's history, a flood so severe that it destroyed a large share of the spring wheat crop in storage on farms as well as much of the standing crops. Entire communities were washed away. Since the deforestation is continuing, the incidence and severity of flooding in Pakistan, India, and Bangladesh seems certain to worsen in the future. In effect, deforestation, particularly in Nepal, where many of the major rivers originate, may be undermining the food producing capability of a subcontinent on which nearly three-quarters of a billion people now depend.

These are only a few of the many examples that could be cited of situations throughout the world where the pressures of a continuously growing demand for food are beginning to undermine the food producing ecosystems. The time has come to inventory systematically these ecological stresses at the global level. Two generalizations concerning agricultural stresses on the ecosystem are indisputable. The situation is certain to worsen in the years immediately ahead, and future world food production prospects will be affected.

Discovering the Earth's Limits

The more conscious we become of various ecological stresses unfolding before us, the more we realize how little we know about the natural system and resources on which our existence depends. The frontiers of ignorance are expanding rapidly. We know little about the consequences of our actions. More often than not, the earth's limits are discovered after the fact, as appears to be the case with the anchovy fishery. All too often the complexity of ecological disasters is such that we confuse symptoms and causes. The risk is that these incorrect or incomplete analyses may lead to a treating of the symptoms rather than the causes of the problem, possibly worsening it in the process.

There are innumerable questions that need to be asked, but even asking the right questions becomes a formidable challenge. At what point does progressive deforestation of the earth begin to alter global climatic patterns? How many species of animal life, ranging from soil microorganisms to predatory birds, can be eliminated from the web of life before the web of life begins to change in unforeseen and perhaps threatening ways?

Which of man's activities are beginning to interrupt some of the natural elemental cycles, such as those for sulfur, oxygen, nitrogen, and carbon? To what extent is the decline of the oceanic fish catch in several major fisheries a product of pollution, to what extent a product of overfishing? At what point do pollution levels in the oceans, now used by man as the ultimate sink, begin to impair their capacity to sustain the complex oceanic web of life which yielded 70 million tons of fish in 1970?

At what point do rising levels of particulate matter in the atmosphere begin to reduce the influx of solar energy, contributing to a possible cooling of the earth? At what point do levels of heavy metal (such as lead) circulating through the ecosystem become a persistent global health threat?

These are the questions that are now before mankind. The United Nations Environmental Program under the leadership of Maurice Strong is designing a monitoring system that will continually observe and measure a great number of physical parameters to determine whether changes in the natural system are occurring, what the long-term consequences of these changes might be, and, if possible, whether human activity is responsible for these changes. But when we learn of situations where man is altering the system through his action and altering it in a way which is not desirable, there is no assurance that an intelligent response will be possible. At present we lack the policy, the institutions, and perhaps even the will to respond adequately to emerging threats.

6

Dependence on Common Global Resources

Not only is pressure on global resources mounting, but the daily headlines also remind us that all countries are increasingly dependent on common resources. With population growth and economic modernization, the requirement for raw materials grows steadily. No country contains within its boundaries all the raw materials it needs. Aside from certain raw materials concentrated in a few geographic locations, we are also dependent upon a common global climatic system, a global hydrological cycle, and a global waste absorptive system. The phenomenal growth in international trade in recent decades reflects in part the rising dependence upon common resources.

A Common Hydrological Cycle

One essential resource that is beginning to affect the expansion of both agricultural and industrial activity in substantial areas of the world is fresh water. Within agriculture its scarcity is now the principal constraint on the spread of the new high-yield dwarf wheats of the Green Revolution in countries ranging from Mexico to Afghanistan. It is hamstringing Soviet efforts to meet expanding consumer demand for more livestock products. In the Northern Hemisphere, industrial activity is being curbed in many locations by the limited capacity of existing lakes and streams to absorb industrial wastes.

Looking ahead, one can see only growing scarcity for this most basic of resources. Water rationing could become commonplace in communities throughout the world as both population growth and spreading affluence press against locally available supplies.

With prospects for the massive desalting of sea water not hopeful for at least the foreseeable future, man continues to be dependent on the natural hydrological cycle. The key question is where growing demand will lead in terms of interventions in this cycle. The amount of fresh water that the cycle produces cannot easily be altered, since it is determined primarily by the influx of solar energy that fuels it. But technologies can be used to manipulate its distribution. We do now have the technologies to cause it to rain in some situations where it otherwise would not. Major rivers can be rerouted and redirected. The combination of growing demand pressures and advancing technologies is shifting the prospect of meteorological aggression from the pages of science fiction to the day-to-day conduct of international affairs.

Competition for waters of various rivers and river systems that cross national boundaries has become intense in recent decades. India and Pakistan required several years to negotiate mutual rights in the allocation of the Indus River waters. Competition between Israel and the Arab countries for the water of the Jordan River is intense. Protracted negotiations were required to allocate the Nile waters between Sudan and Egypt. Use of the Colorado River waters continues to be a thorn in the side of relations between the United States and Mexico.

Soviet efforts to expand domestic food supplies have been seriously handicapped by a scarcity of fresh water. When the Virgin Lands project of the late 1950s failed to live up to expectations, the Soviets attempted to expand their food supply by intensifying production on existing cultivated areas. The consequent need for more water led them seriously to consider diverting southward the flow of four major rivers that now flow north into the Arctic Ocean. Once these plans became public, however, the international meteorological community was quick to respond. Meteorologists urged the Soviets to abandon these plans, arguing that to interrupt this flow of warm water into the Arctic would alter the climate in the Arctic, and in turn trigger compensatory adjustments throughout the global climatic system. One study estimated that rainfall in central North America would be measurably reduced if the Soviets were to proceed with these plans.

In late 1973, it was reported that construction had begun on a

175-mile canal to divert a portion of the waters of two Siberian rivers into arid central Asia. If the Soviets proceed with the project, it may be decades before the full water diversion plan is implemented. In the meantime, Soviet perceptions of the dependability of its grain import supplies—most of which must come from the United States—may help shape the government's decision as to whether or not to carry through such an expensive, meteorologically risky program.

In the United States, there are now rain-making firms that will contract their services to national governments, local governments, farmers' associations, or any other concerns willing to pay for their services. A few years ago, the state of Florida contracted with a rain-making firm to increase rainfall in Florida in order to break an extended drought that was damaging agricultural crops and threatening wildlife in the Everglades. In this case, the rainfall gained through atmospheric intervention was at the expense of the surrounding ocean. But the interesting question is: What if Texas were to sign such a rain-making contract? How would this affect relations between the United States and Mexico? That this type of international conflict has become a pressing possibility was underscored in December 1973, when Rhodesia initiated a nationwide cloud-seeding operation which, authorities hoped, would increase the country's rainfall by at least 10 percent. If the plan is successful, it can only be so at the expense of neighboring African nations, whose share of the region's rainfall will be reduced.

The Food and Agriculture Organization projects that global demand for fresh water will increase 240 percent by the end of the century. Needless to say, this could generate great pressures on countries to use whatever technologies are available or can be developed to expand their fresh-water supplies. Since national efforts to expand fresh water supplies by using advanced technologies often have transnational if not global consequences, the international community must seriously consider regulating national interventions in the climatic system.

The Scramble for Marine Protein

The world catch of a large number of the leading commercial species of table-grade fish now exceeds the estimated sustainable catch. The result is declining stocks for such key species as tuna, herring, cod, and ocean perch in the north Atlantic and anchovies in the southeast Pacific. Each year the list of overfished species lengthens. In an unregulated situation, the natural course of events is for each fishery to expand beyond its sustainable catch, eventually leading to its collapse. There are now instances on record, several of them in the northwest Atlantic, where stocks of minor species have been virtually wiped out. Even with the necessary international cooperation, it may take years or even decades for the more severely depleted stocks to recover.

The increasingly intense competition in ocean fisheries is reflected in the rising frequency of conflicts among countries. Among these are the cod war between NATO allies, Iceland and Great Britain, resulting from Iceland's extension of its offshore limits to fifty miles. Soviet fishing vessels have been seized by the U.S. Coast Guard within the U.S. twelve-mile territorial limits off the coast of Alaska. The state of Massachusetts is threatening to extend its offshore limits to two hundred miles in an effort to salvage what remains of its fishing industry.

The tuna war waged off the west coast of Latin America is longstanding. During a recent twelve-month period, the Ecuadorian navy seized and fined fifty-six U.S. tuna trawlers caught within Ecuador's unilaterally established two hundred-mile offshore limit. Competition between the expanding Soviet and Japanese fishing fleets in the north Pacific manifests itself in frequent clashes.

Exactly how the catch of various species should be allocated among countries can be an exceedingly complex matter. The greater the number of countries involved and the more varied they are economically, the more difficult finding an acceptable formula is likely to be. Formulas may be derived from historical shares, coastal proximity, size of fleet, size of population, protein needs, or some combination thereof.

Among the earliest efforts to sort through this politically sticky set of issues is that occurring within the International Commission for Northwest Atlantic Fisheries, a group of fifteen countries actively engaged in fishing in the area, which has organized to protect the fisheries from Rhode Island northward along the North American coast to Greenland. Among other things, the commission proposes to member governments joint regulatory actions designed to keep stocks at levels permitting maximum sustainable yields. The over-all quotas established are often far below the catch of recent years. Fishing for some species in selected subregions has been banned.

National shares of the over-all quota in the northwest Atlantic are most commonly determined by a formula that allocates 40 percent of the catch according to average catches in the most recent 10 years in the fishery and 40 percent according to those of the most recent three years, with the remainder divided between a preference for coastal countries and an allowance for miscellaneous factors such as new entrants into the fishery and the catch of non-member nations. Thus far the commission has a mixed record. Not infrequently, one or more of the fifteen member countries refuses to comply with commission recommendations, thereby rendering them useless. Inability to get a consensus on a recommendation to restrict the salmon catch has caused stocks to deteriorate to the point where Canada has proposed an absolute ban on salmon fishing. Future conflicts can be expected as the United States urges relative newcomers to the area to limit their fishing efforts in order to avert a continuing decline in its share of the region's yield.

Most successful agreements to limit and allocate catches to date have occurred among industrial countries in the more intensely worked northern fisheries. Even here Iceland has broken ranks by extending its offshore limits to fifty miles. Of relatively minor over-all economic importance to the United States or European industrial countries, fishing is of crucial importance to the Icelandic economy, where it accounts for 80 percent of export earnings. Two successive devaluations of the krona were tied to poor catches in 1967 and 1968.

Competition among countries for this valuable and finite resource is keen. The wealthier countries such as the Soviet Union, Japan, and, to a lesser extent, the United States are investing huge sums in fishing fleets and new technologies such as sonar, which permit them to roam the oceans taking fish wherever they can be found. For the poor countries with a desperate need for protein, this poses a serious problem. Lacking the capital and technology to compete on these terms, many are extending their territorial limits beyond the traditional and widely accepted twelve miles in an effort to obtain a more satisfactory share of the world's marine protein supply.

The years ahead may well witness a continuing decline in the global catch per capita of table-grade fish. Should the catch fail to meet the additional demand generated by population growth, the impact on prices and nutrition will be felt by consumers everywhere. International competition and conflict over limited supplies will inevitably grow. Consumers everywhere have an important stake in the UN Law of the Sea Conference, which began in late 1973, where an effort will be made to evolve a cooperative international approach for the management of ocean fisheries.

Overloaded Waste Absorptive Capacity

We have been slow to realize that the earth's capacity to absorb the various wastes and by-products of human economic activity is also finite and that this capacity is, in effect, a "resource" that can and ultimately must be dealt with on a global basis too. Countries that are highly industrialized have generally now reached the point where they have exploited this resource beyond an acceptable sustainable level.

The unwillingness of populations in affluent areas to bear the environmental consequence of excess waste discharge has resulted in the passage of a vast amount of legislation in recent years limiting the waste discharge of industrial and other activities. Within the United States, this includes national legislation such as the Clean Air Act, the Clean Water Act, legislation in almost every state, and ordinances at the local level. The net effect of compliance with these new laws is to raise the cost of production, particularly in some of the more pollution intensive industries.

One consequence of the awakening of popular opinion to the perils of growing environmental stress in the more industrialized countries is the emergence of a trend among high-polluting industries to side-step the problem by locating new plants in areas of the world with less stringent environmental control legislation. Some developing nations, in turn, are beginning to perceive their underutilized waste absorptive capacity as a resource to be exploited in competitive efforts to attract new investment by multinational corporations. Many poorer nations are willing, up to a point at least, to trade the cleanliness of their air and water in order to raise the low economic level of their populations. In effect, they are proposing to "export" their willingness and ability to absorb economic waste products.

Brazil, for example, has publicly invited corporations in pollution intensive industries to locate their plants in Brazil, where there is as yet relatively little pollution outside the major cities, and where there are few pollution regulations. Caribbean nations have attracted various heavy industries, particularly oil refineries, which have been unable or unwilling to meet the high costs of complying with environmental regulations in the United States. Japanese industrialists, faced with perhaps the world's most serious national pollution problem, are beginning to locate pollution intensive activities elsewhere, particularly in poorer Asian nations.

When the ecological consequences of economic activity are local in nature, individual countries must make their own decisions on the difficult trade-offs between economic activity and environmental quality. Where the discharge of wastes has adverse international consequences, however, as in the case of ocean pollution, international control and pollution standards are called for. In this critical area, an increase in aid resources from the richer nations to the poor nations may be necessary to help finance pollution abatement equipment, which the poor nations might otherwise view as not worth the price.

Food: North American Dominance

Beyond the dependence on common supplies of marine protein, most countries also depend on exportable surpluses of food from only a few countries. Over the past few decades, world patterns of grain trade have been dramatically altered. Geographic regions once producing large exportable surpluses of food in the 1930s, such as Latin America and Eastern Europe, including the Soviet Union, no longer have such surpluses. Four decades ago, Latin America and North America were exporting virtually identical amounts of grain. Since then, explosive population growth has converted Latin America into a net cereal importer in some recent years.

⋅ North America (the United States and Canada) and Australia are the only geographic regions now producing regional food surpluses. The United States is not only the world's major exporter of wheat and feed grains, it is now the leading exporter of rice as well. Indeed, North America now controls a greater share of the world's exportable

Table 9. The Changing Pattern of World Grain Trade

REGION	1934–38	1948–52	1960	1966	1973 (prel.) (fiscal year)
			(million metric tons)		
North America	+5	+23	+39	+59	+88
Latin America	+9	+1	0	+5	−4
Western Europe	−24	−22	−25	−27	−21
Eastern Europe & USSR	+5	—	0	−4	−27
Africa	+1	0	−2	−7	−4
Asia	+2	−6	−17	−34	−39
Australia	+3	+3	+6	+8	+7

SOURCE: Based on U.S. Department of Agriculture data.
NOTE: Plus = net exports; minus = net imports.

grain supplies than the Middle East does of oil.

The world now depends on the United States for nearly 90 percent of the exportable supplies of soybeans, a leading global source of protein. A decision by the United States to curb soybean exports directly and dramatically affects soybean supplies and prices throughout the world. Mainland China was the dominant supplier of soybeans in the 1930s, providing 90 percent of all soybeans entering world markets. Continuing population growth in an already densely populated country has absorbed both the growth in production and the exportable surplus, converting mainland China into a soybean importer in 1973.

Apart from political whims in the United States that make growing dependence of the rest of the world on U.S. food supplies a high-risk situation, there is also a substantial climatic risk involved. The United States and Canada are subject to the same climatic influences and share a North American history of twenty-year drought cycles going back over the century or so of recorded data.

Energy: Middle Eastern Control

As energy consumption rises, the flow of energy fuels from areas of supply to those of consumption swells, greatly increasing the share of world energy supply that crosses national boundaries. In 1925, only 14 percent of the world's energy fuels crossed national boundaries; as of the mid-1970s, this share exceeds one-third and is climbing rapidly.

Relatively few of the world's 160 nation-states are self-sufficient in energy fuels. The vast majority look to imports for some if not most of their energy needs. Only a handful—Saudi Arabia, Venezuela, Algeria, Indonesia, Libya, Kuwait, Iran, Iraq, Nigeria, and a few others—are significant net energy exporters. Japan depends on imports for 99 percent of its petroleum needs. Western Europe is only slightly less dependent, importing 96 percent of its petroleum.

As petroleum consumption in the United States, the world's leading energy consumer, continues its exponential growth of 3 to 4 percent per year, consumption is steadily outpacing production, converting the United States from a position of marginal dependence on imports to major dependence. The production of crude oil within the continental United States peaked in 1970 and has been declining since. Alaskan oil, due to come into the market within the next few years, is expected to offset almost exactly the production decline in the forty-eight contiguous states. Assuming that consumption continues to climb, it is anticipated that the gap will widen steadily until, by 1985, the United States will be dependent on foreign sources for well over half of its petroleum supplies. New efforts to develop alternative energy sources and slow the growth of domestic demand may reduce the increase in dependence on imports below that projected level.

The massive projected petroleum imports into the United States, Europe, and Japan mean growing competition for exportable supplies throughout the world. This, combined with the willingness of exporting countries to restrict production and exports, translates into sharply higher prices for gasoline, petroleum, and fuel oil.

Minerals: The Developing Countries

As noted earlier, no country or continent is endowed with all the raw materials needed by a modern industrial society. The geologist Preston Cloud points out that "no part of the earth, not even on a continent-wide basis, is self-sufficient in critical metals. North America is relatively rich in molybdenum and poor in tin, tungsten and manganese, for instance, whereas Asia is comparatively rich in tin, tungsten, and manganese, and apparently less well supplied with molybdenum. Cuba and New Caledonia have well over half of the world's total known reserves of nickel. The main known reserves of cobalt are in the Republic of the Congo [Zaire], Cuba, New Caledonia and parts of Asia."

Interdependence among nations is commonly viewed in terms of

Table 10. World Proven Crude Oil Reserves, 1972

	BILLIONS OF BARRELS	PERCENT OF TOTAL
Middle East	356	53
Africa	106	16
USSR, Eastern Europe, and China (est.)	98	15
North America	53	8
Latin America	33	5
Far East and Australia	15	2
Western Europe	9	1
Total	670	100

SOURCE: *Middle East Economic Digest*, October 1973.

dependence of poor countries on rich ones. And so it is with capital and technology. But with minerals, dependence of rich countries on poor ones is far greater and increasing year by year. Those countries that industrialized earliest are depleting their indigenous supplies of many of the basic raw materials required by modern industry. As a result, industrial countries, including particularly the United States, Japan, and those of Western Europe, are becoming increasingly dependent on the remaining mineral reserves of the world, which are located largely in pre-industrial countries. Western European consumption of eleven basic industrial raw materials (bauxite, copper, lead, phosphate, zinc, chrome ore, manganese ore, magnesium, nickel, tungsten, and tin) exceeds production. In fact, nearly all needs for copper, phosphate, tin, nickel, manganese ore, and chrome ore must now be met from imports.

Dependence of the United States on imported raw materials is increasing steadily. Of the thirteen basic industrial raw materials required by its modern economy, the United States in 1950 was dependent on imports for more than half of its supplies of four—aluminum, manganese, nickel, and tin. Projections by the Department of the Interior indicate that the United States will depend on imports for more than half of its supplies of nine of this group of raw materials by 1985. The new additions to the list are iron, lead, tungsten, chromium, and zinc (see Table II). The growing requirements of the U.S. economy, with its enormous capacity for consuming raw materials, will contribute to increasing competition among countries for existing raw material supplies.

The prospect of collective bargaining by raw material countries is a very real one in those instances where a few countries control most of the world's exportable supplies and where the practicality of substituting other raw materials is limited. For example, four developing countries—Chile, Peru, Zambia, and Zaire—now supply most of the world's exportable surplus of copper. Three others—Malaysia, Bolivia, and Thailand—account for 70 percent of all tin entering international trade channels. Australia, Mexico, and Peru account for 60 percent of the supply of lead.

Mineral reserves are important to agriculture as well as to industry. Of the three principal nutrients in chemical fertilizer—nitrogen, phosphate, and potash—the first is available in virtually endless amounts in the atmosphere, but supplies of the latter two require mining underground reserves. Unfortunately, the world supply of these two minerals is concentrated in a very few locations. Canada has most of the world's known reserves of potash within its borders. The United States, Morocco, and Tunisia account for most of the phosphate

Table 11. U.S. Dependence on Imports of Principal Industrial
Raw Materials with Projections to 2000

RAW MATERIAL	1950	1970	1985	2000
		(percent imported)		
Aluminum	64	85	96	98
Chromium	n.a.	100	100	100
Copper	31	0	34	56
Iron	8	30	55	67
Lead	39	31	62	67
Manganese	88	95	100	100
Nickel	94	90	88	89
Phosphorus	8	0	0	2
Potassium	14	42	47	61
Sulfur	2	0	28	52
Tin	77	n.a.	100	100
Tungsten	n.a.	50	87	97
Zinc	38	59	72	84

SOURCE: Data are derived from U.S. Department of the Interior publications.

entering international trade. Since the overwhelming majority of countries are dependent upon imports for most if not all of their supplies of plant nutrients, their internally produced food supply is dependent to that degree on external supplies.

Consequences of Interdependence

An understanding of the growing interaction and interdependence among countries brought by dependence on common global resources is central to our understanding of international relations in the years ahead. Resource scarcities are altering the economic and political relationships among countries, changing the relative position and influence of countries in the international hierarchy. A given country may find its position abruptly strengthened in one sector of economic activity and weakened in another. World food scarcity has greatly improved the terms on which the United States makes foodstuffs available to the rest of the world, but its negotiating position with respect to many other raw materials in the world economy has deteriorated sharply. The converse is true for the Soviet Union, which is highly vulnerable in the food sector but in a commanding position with energy, which it still produces in surplus.

Efforts by individual countries to expand their share of global output, employment, and wealth are taking new forms. Linkages between global scarcities and internal policies affecting economic growth, inflation, and employment are becoming both more numerous and more direct. In the mid-1970s, a new global politics of resource scarcity is emerging.

7

The Global Politics
of Resource Scarcity

The exponential expansion of global economic activity against the backdrop of increasing environmental stresses and resource scarcities is compelling mankind to address in a new context the issue of how resources and economic activity are distributed among countries. As long as the supply of a given resource could always be expanded, the share consumed by any one country was of little concern to other countries. As long as the prospects of economic growth appeared to be virtually limitless, the rich could urge the poor at home and abroad to wait, arguing that the benefits of growth would eventually trickle down. But when the point is reached where over-all economic output or the supply of a particular resource can no longer be easily or quickly expanded, then the focus shifts from expanding the pie to dividing the pie.

Dividing the Pie

The difficult adjustments that must be made in economic systems, both domestic and international, are immensely easier in a rapidly growing economy than in a slowly growing or static one. But given what we know and can foresee at present about the availability of resources and the state of the environment, it may be possible to achieve an acceptable level of living for everyone in the world only by slowing the growth in consumption of material goods among the rich countries, while accelerating it among the poor.

Traditionally, rates of economic growth in non-industrial societies were closely tied to those in the industrial countries. In part, this was because rates of economic growth in non-industrial countries often correlated closely with growth in their export earnings. The close correlation in growth rates between the two groups of countries may be diminishing. Control of the lion's share of world exportable supplies of many raw materials, ranging from petroleum to several key minerals, is giving the non-industrial countries leverage in the international economic system which they have not heretofore enjoyed. The terms on which they make resources available are influenced strongly by their desire to attain a more equitable share of the global economic pie.

Numerous efforts are under way by less developed countries to use their newly acquired bargaining power to increase the share of processing in raw material exports. Poor countries seem anxious to abandon as rapidly as possible their traditional "hewers of wood, drawers of water" role in the world economy. For example, Turkey and Japan have made an agreement whereby Japan is building a 50,000-ton-per-year ferrochrome alloy plant in exchange for a million tons of chrome ore to be delivered over a ten-year period.

If the Shah of Iran gets his way, more and more of the oil leaving Iran will be refined rather than crude oil. Argentina, Brazil, and India are taking advantage of the global scarcity of cattle hides by restricting or banning exports, thus furthering development of their domestic leather goods industry. In effect, they hope to shift the geographic focus of the leather goods export industry from Italy and Japan to the Southern Hemisphere. Indonesia is combining its favorable resource situation with mounting Japanese fears of pollution at home to persuade Japanese firms investing in mineral extraction to ship processed ore rather than crude ore to Japan. The oil exporting nations, particularly Saudi Arabia and Iran, have begun trading the assurance of energy supplies to selected countries in return for industrial investments within their borders.

Increasingly the poor countries are invoking the need for greater social justice at the international level in their economic relationships with the rich countries. Algeria took over control of the French oil and gas interests in the Algerian Sahara with the express desire of providing an acceptable level of living for every family in Algeria. The Algerians believed that if these resources remained in French hands, this objective would not be fulfilled.

In Chile, the late President Allende linked the terms of compensation to the copper firms whose holdings his government had expropriated to the needs of the Chilean people. He noted that there were 700,000 children in his country who will never develop their full physical and mental potential because they were deprived of sufficient protein in the early years of life. Foreign based copper mining companies, he argued, have invested a paltry sum in Chile, but have taken out enough profits to fill the protein deficit in Chile for as far as one can see into the future.

Peru's former Foreign Minister Edgardo Mercado Jarrin justified the extension of his country's offshore limits to two hundred miles in terms of Peru's needs for fish from the rich fishing grounds off the coast of Peru which provided much of the protein consumed by the Peruvian people and earn most of the country's foreign exchange. He argued that industrial countries such as the Soviet Union, Japan, and the United States are able to invest in sophisticated technologies such as sonar, floating fish processing factories, and auxiliary fishing fleets. Peru, on the other hand, lacks the capital and technology to compete in these ways. It can protect its share of the world protein supply only by extending its offshore limits. Political leaders in other maritime developing countries are taking similar positions.

Access: The New Imperative

Since World War II, the overriding objective of national trade policies has been to expand access to markets abroad for export products. The General Agreement on Tariffs and Trade (GATT) was created specifically with this in mind. Five successive rounds of GATT negotiations since World War II have steadily reduced tariff barriers, as evidenced by the healthy growth in world trade throughout the postwar period.

Scarcity is now focusing attention on another kind of access—the access to needed supplies. This issue is a particularly urgent one because of the recent and growing tendency for countries to limit exports of raw materials for unprecedented reasons that have taken trading partners by surprise—to cope with internal inflationary pressures, to extend the foreign exchange earning lifetime of a non-renewable resource, to increase the share of indigenous processing, to improve export terms, or perhaps to take advantage of anticipated future price rises.

Countries with non-renewable resources such as petroleum and minerals are beginning to ask themselves at what rate they want to exploit their resources. During that long period of history when potential supplies far exceeded anticipated demand, supplier countries were eager to maximize exports, and the issue of rate of exploitation was seldom raised. Today, policy-making in this area is much more complex. What should determine the rate at which Venezuela's remaining oil reserves are exploited—its own longer-term foreign exchange needs or the short-term consumption needs of the United States? The former may argue for a much lower level of petroleum production and export than the latter.

The number of countries banning or restricting exports of scarce commodities in order to cope with internal inflationary pressures is growing. Brazil limited the export of beef in 1973 to levels 30 percent below the corresponding month in 1972. Thailand, a leading world supplier of rice, banned exports for several months in 1973 in order to prevent inordinate price rises in its national food staple. The United States limited the export of soybeans during the summer of 1973, even though it is virtually the sole supplier of this critical protein resource to the rest of the world.

The United States, a leading exporter of forest products, is responding to soaring lumber prices by attempting to negotiate a voluntary import quota with Japan on purchases of American forest products. This represents a dramatic turnabout in the American-Japanese trading relationship, since the focus over the past decade has been on the negotiation of voluntary quotas with Tokyo to limit Japanese exports of textiles and steel to the United States. Under what conditions should a country be permitted to use trade policy to limit or ban the export of a scarce good and thus, in effect, to export inflation?

Guidelines governing terms of access to external markets and penalties for those countries that fail to comply have evolved within the framework of GATT, but there are no such guidelines on whether or when a country should be permitted to withhold a given resource. We must begin at least to ask the question of how to cope with export limitations on raw materials which directly affect the well-being of people throughout the world.

Collective Bargaining by Exporters

In the wake of the extraordinarily successful, highly visible collective bargaining by petroleum exporters over the past few years, the possibility of collective bargaining by suppliers of other raw materials is being viewed with more than ordinary interest. Suppliers of some raw materials are certain to attempt to emulate the Organization of Petroleum Exporting Countries (OPEC). The four copper exporting countries are already doing so. There is concern within the aluminum industry that the politics of petroleum are becoming the politics of bauxite. Coffee exporters are now beginning to bargain collectively as a group, whereas in the past they were dependent on the willingness of the importing countries to support prices of coffee. The prospects for successful collective negotiation by raw material exporters are influenced by a number of factors, including the number of suppliers, the ability and willingness to restrict supply, the availability of possible substitutes, alternative sources of foreign exchange earnings for the supplier, and the possibility for collective bargaining by importing countries.

Efforts to bargain collectively fail far more often than they succeed, but a convergence of special circumstances can give the exporting countries the leverage to alter the terms on which a given raw material is made available. A prolonged strike in the mining or transport sector and interference with global transport arteries, such as blockage of the Suez Canal or the severing of a strategic rail or pipeline linking a major supplier with world markets, are but a few of the events which can combine to strengthen inadvertently the hands of exporting countries.

Perhaps the dominant factor influencing the prospects for successful bargaining by suppliers is the changing tempo in the world marketplace. Exponential demand curves are affecting the marketplace for raw materials, creating a psychology of scarcity and of speculation. A bullish world market for a given commodity makes it much easier for its exporters to bargain, either individually or collectively, than when it is in chronic oversupply. Awareness that many of the earth's resources are limited and exhaustible is rising, in many instances converting markets which have traditionally been buyers' markets into sellers' markets.

Rethinking Development: The Rich

Global resource scarcities have a heavy impact on economic and political relationships among nations, in part because they affect so directly the living conditions within individual countries. They affect the very life styles of people, their dietary habits, their mode of transportation. The levels of protein intake in the Soviet Union, Japan, and

Bangladesh are directly affected by U.S. farm export policies. The level of thermostats and size of automobiles in the United States is inevitably influenced by production decisions of Middle Eastern oil countries. It is this dimension of global resource scarcity that makes the terms of access to needed resources at the international level such a politically sensitive issue.

The relationship between life styles in individual countries and global resource scarcity is becoming increasingly evident. It has long been part of the conventional wisdom within the international development community that the two billion people living in the poor countries could not aspire to the life style enjoyed by the average North American because there was not enough iron ore, petroleum, and protein in the world to provide it. But even while accepting this, most of us in the United States have continued the pursuit of superaffluence, increasing our consumption of resources as though there were no limit to the amount that could be consumed.

Political leaders in the poor countries are beginning to ask why a small segment of mankind living in the rich countries should be permitted to consume such a disproportionately large share of the earth's resources. What right have Americans, now only 5 percent of the world's people, to consume nearly a third of the earth's energy and minerals? This question is being raised in the various international forums where access to and allocation of resources among countries is discussed.

Within affluent societies, the presumed link between levels of well-being and the volume of material consumption needs to be carefully examined. There is growing evidence that this relationship is at best a tenuous one. At low levels of income and consumption, an increase in material goods consumption does very much affect one's level of well-being, but after a point improvements in satisfaction are scarcely perceptible. Will a 20 percent increase in income for the more affluent among us bring a 20 percent increase in well-being, a 10 percent increase, or any improvement at all? For a man with only a crust of bread, the acquisition of a second crust greatly improves his well-being. For a man with a loaf of bread, an additional crust has little effect.

The technologies underlying modern economic systems evolved in a situation of relative abundance. Land, water, energy, and other resources were abundant and cheap. But now there is a need to reexamine these technologies in the light of growing resource scarcity. Could current levels of individual mobility be retained with a much lower level of resource use merely by limiting the size of automobiles? Could energy consumption be greatly reduced with a properly de-

signed public transport system? Should contractors be building sky-
scrapers, with their enormous energy requirements, or should we
abandon the competition to see who can build the tallest building in
each major city?

The regulation of the size of automobiles in the United States,
limiting size to, say, the 2,500 pounds of subcompacts, is long over-
due. This single step would simultaneously contribute to the solution
of several U.S. development problems. It would reduce the need for
most, though not all, current energy imports, freeing energy resources
for more needy countries. The reduced automobile size would diminish the amount of raw materials used in automobile manufacture,
sharply reduce air pollution, and have the effect of increasing parking
space by a third. The net effect would be a more mobile U.S. population, a stronger dollar, lower prices for gasoline, and a healtheir U.S.
population.

If Americans persist in driving large automobiles, it may help drive
up the world price of energy further, pushing it beyond the reach of
many of the world's low income users. A doubling in the world price
of petroleum may mean that a small farmer in northern India with
six acres of land and a small irrigation pump may no longer be able
to afford fuel for his pump. The continuous pursuit of superaffluence
by some of us in a world of scarce resources can now directly affect
the prospects for survival elsewhere.

Since the contrasts in food consumption levels among countries are
so great, thought needs to be given to how diets could be simplified
in the wealthy nations in order to reduce per capita claims on the
earth's scarce resources of land and water. What are the possibilities
of substituting less costly, more efficient forms of protein for, say,
beef?

Consumption patterns in the United States suggest that there are
two broad approaches to reducing per capita resource requirements
for food. One is to substitute vegetable oils for animal fat; the other
is to substitute vegetable protein for animal protein.

Over the past three decades, vegetable oils have been extensively
replacing animal fats in the American diet. In 1940, for example, the
average American consumed 17 pounds of butter and 2 pounds of
margarine. By 1971, the average American was consuming 11 pounds
of margarine and 5 pounds of butter. Lard has been almost pushed
off supermarket shelves by the hydrogenated vegetable shortenings.
At least 65 percent of the whipped toppings and more than 35 percent
of the coffee whiteners in the United States today are of non-dairy
origin. This trend reduces both per capita good costs and per capita
claims on agricultural resources, and it reduces the intake of saturated

animal fats now widely believed to be a factor contributing to heart disease.

Technology for the substitution of vegetable for animal proteins has made considerable progress, mainly in the area of soya-based meat substitutes. The development of a technique for spinning soya protein into fibers, duplicating the spinning of synthetic textile fibers, permits the close emulation of the fibrous qualities of meat. Food technologists can now compress soya fibers into meat form and, with the appropriate flavoring and coloring, come up with reasonable substitutes for beef, pork, and poultry. With livestock protein, particularly beef, becoming more costly, this technique is likely to gain a strong commercial foothold in the near future.

The greatest single area of protein substitution promises to be the use of vegetable protein to augment meat proteins in ground meats. Soya protein "extenders" are being added to a variety of processed and ground meat products, frequently improving flavor, cooking qualities, and nutrition as well as reducing prices. Soya protein extenders are already widely used in institutions throughout the United States, and supermarket sales to the public have also begun—a trend that deserves encouragement through research budgets and nutritional education programs. There are now strong economical, ecological, and nutritional reasons for moving in this direction.

The production of a pound of poultry or pork requires substantially less grain and high protein feeds than the production of a pound of beef. Per capita pressures on resources, then, can also be reduced somewhat by shifting consumption away from beef toward these less costly animal products.

Rethinking Development: The Poor

Within the developing nations, the prospect of global resource scarcity calls for major rethinking of development strategies. Just as the rich nations can no longer pursue their present patterns of resource-wasting growth, the poor nations must cease to think in terms of an undiscriminating emulation of the habits and technologies of the rich nations. Developing nations must select carefully from available technological and social patterns to find those most suited to their own genuine future needs. In some cases, unique approaches may be necessary. The basic challenge for the poorer nations is to design a development strategy that will provide a relatively satisfactory standard of living with a minimal level of resource consumption.

Within the transportation sector, for example, an imaginative combination of transport technologies selected from the panoply now
available could permit a society at an early stage of economic development to provide a much higher degree of mobility for its people than
is possible by following current fashion and adopting what is essentially the American model. An automobile-centered transport system
in a poor country means that limited budgetary and foreign exchange
resources will be absorbed almost exclusively by the small urban elite
able to afford an automobile. A system that relied heavily on public
transport combined with the mass manufacture of simply designed,
low-cost bicycles and motor scooters would be more socially equitable
and would provide far greater mobility for the population as a whole,
at a given level of energy availability.

Special attention must be given by poor nations to means of providing better nutrition with the lowest possible pressure on the nation's
limited food-producing resources of land, water, and energy. The
widespread consumption of pulses, including particularly soy or other
beans, in combination with adequate grain consumption, provides a
nutritious diet with more economical use of agricultural resources
than a nutritionally comparable diet relying heavily on beef to provide
protein. Among the various livestock proteins, chicken and pork
require far fewer resources to produce than beef.

Given the growing dimensions of the employment problem facing
most poor countries, as well as the growing scarcity and cost of both
physical and energy resources, economic sense dictates a strong emphasis on the use of labor intensive techniques in both industry and
agriculture. In some cases, labor intensive patterns of production have
already proven successful in attaining efficient production at low resource cost. In other cases, research energies must be directed toward
the development of new industrial technologies that will allow developing nations to take best advantage of their abundance of labor. But
even when appropriate technologies are readily available, many governments have failed to follow policies designed to encourage their
use.

As we confront the question of how to satisfy basic human needs
on a small planet with limited resources, we have much to learn from
a number of countries that have pioneered innovative approaches for
providing at a very low resource cost the minimum essentials for
decent living to the large majority of their populations. As discussed
at greater length in Chapter 9, Sri Lanka has done this in the health
field, Singapore in urban housing, and Taiwan in rural development.
The Chinese experience may be particularly interesting in view of the
progress made despite the size, poverty, and relative isolation of China

in recent years. Confronted with the task of improving the welfare of the world's largest population with very limited resources at their disposal, Chinese leaders had to confront the question of allocating scarce resources long before most other nations.

The planned obsolescence of everything from fashions to automobiles built into economic systems in the more affluent nations does not exist in China. A well-developed public transportation system combined with the extensive use of bicycles provides effective personal mobility without the tremendous environmental, mineral, and energy costs of an automobile-based transport system. Through the direct consumption of soybeans and reliance on pork and poultry to the almost total exclusion of beef and dairy products, China has achieved a remarkably high level of nutrition for a nation of 800 million people with a per capita income of perhaps $160 a year.

Unlike many developing countries now experiencing rising levels of unemployment as a result of the postwar population explosion, China has harnessed the energies of its people to undertake some of the most extensive public works projects in human history. Many of these have centered on the development and conservation of water resources. More recently, human labor has been mobilized on a large scale to cope with environmental problems. Millions have participated in projects designed to reforest land that has been denuded over the centuries.

The purpose of these brief comments on China is not to suggest that the Chinese model is necessarily desirable or appropriate for other societies. It is a model that has involved a great deal of control and restriction of individual freedom. What is important is that the Chinese have already found a way to deal with many problems of acute resource scarcity now being faced by other countries, rich and poor alike. It is in this context that the Chinese experience is worth studying by all countries, regardless of their stage of economic development.

As the supply of a particular commodity becomes scarce relative to the demand, we must decide how to achieve a balance between the two. It could be achieved by reliance on the market mechanism, with rising prices reducing demand and then bringing it into balance with the available supply. The disadvantage of this solution is that those who have the least purchasing power sometimes suffer a great deal. If the scarce commodity is food, suffering may be severe, even resulting in widespread death from malnutrition and starvation. An alternative way of balancing supply and demand is through rationing, a practice that is likely to become increasingly prevalent in the years ahead.

Stresses on the International System

Historically, those countries that industrialized first and controlled most of the advanced technology and capital supplies have enjoyed a position of leadership in international affairs. Their economic and political influence has been strong. In economic relationships between these countries and the non-industrial countries, the terms of trade have, until recently, rather consistently favored the industrial countries. Technological superiority and economic power have readily converted into political influence.

As of the mid-1970s, basic shifts in economic and political relationships are occurring among the industrial and less developed countries. In large measure, this can be traced to the growing dependence of the countries that industrialized earliest on imports of energy fuels and raw materials and on the growing global scarcity of many raw materials. The result has been a dramatic shift of economic power to some raw material suppliers.

The growth in bargaining power of the exporting nations has brought with it a rather massive transfer of resources from the industrial or more developed countries to some of the less developed countries, particularly the pre-industrial oil exporting countries. Unfortunately, the distribution of oil reserves in the developing nations is very uneven. Half of the world's exportable oil supplies are contained in three countries, Saudi Arabia, Kuwait, and Libya, which have a combined population little larger than that of New York City.

The shift in the world energy market from a buyer's to a seller's market, combined with the discovery by the exporters that they could bargain collectively with great success, occurred almost overnight during the mid-1970s. Saudi Arabia, the world's leading energy exporter, has been the first pre-industrial country to become a superpower. It wields great influence today in international economic and political affairs. The new-found power of the oil exporting countries derives not only from the great dependence of most leading industrial countries on imported energy but also from the fact that the exporting countries, which have large oil exports and few people, are rapidly accumulating vast financial reserves. The wealth buildup in the principal oil exporting countries is occurring with a rapidity and on a scale without precedent. The oil proceeds of eleven OPEC members are expected to rise from $22 billion in 1973 to $85 billion in 1974. What they do with their new foreign exchange reserves, how they decide to use them, will have a great impact on the world economy and on the international monetary system.

While some of the less developed countries are benefiting handsomely from this abrupt shift in the terms of trade between the raw material exporters and the exporters of industrial products, others are suffering greatly. The redistribution of wealth taking place means that the third world cannot be considered an economically homogeneous area. For those less developed countries which are importers of both energy and food as well as fertilizer, the tripling of world energy and food prices between mid-1972 and the end of 1973, and the simultaneous doubling of international fertilizer prices, brought great hardship which has yet to be fully assessed. Global scarcity of these critical resources seriously threatens the future economic progress of those countries that are densely populated and not blessed with any of the critical raw materials the rest of the world needs.

The impact of soaring energy prices on industrial countries is largely a matter of inconvenience and modest cutbacks in some of the luxury uses of energy. But for the poor countries there is little fat to be pared. Most cuts in energy use will quickly hit the bone, affecting the levels of industrial output and employment. These countries do not have air conditioners and large automobiles which can be turned off or slowed down in order to conserve energy.

The convulsive changes in the world energy and food economies occurring during the mid-1970s are putting great stress on both the international economic system and national political systems. Runaway inflation, soaring prices, spreading unemployment, and shrinking levels of economic activity will almost certainly lead to social unrest and political unrest, particularly but not only in the less developed countries. The cumulative impact of higher energy and food prices during the mid-1970s is likely to topple many governments.

As the newly rich, pre-industrial countries learn how to use their new political influence, it will trigger efforts by other countries, both industrial and pre-industrial, to seek new means of redressing the changing power relationships. Countries will strive to find new ways of using national monetary, fiscal, trade, and investment policies either to protect the international economic status quo or to acquire a larger share of the world's wealth.

8

Population Growth and the Human Condition

In reality, our world today is two worlds, one rich, one poor; one literate, one largely illiterate; one overfed and overweight, one hungry and malnourished; one affluent and consumption-oriented, one poverty-stricken and subsistence-oriented. For the economically advanced, life expectancy at birth closely approaches the biblical threescore and ten. In the developing countries, millions do not survive infancy. In one world, self-sustaining economic growth has permitted successive improvements in human welfare; in the other, all too many are locked into self-perpetuating cycles of poverty and misery.

Population growth, in itself, is almost never the sole cause of poverty. A reduced rate of population growth will not assure a rapid improvement in individual well-being, though it will make its attainment easier. A few countries have managed to sustain a high rate of growth in national product despite rapid population growth. Nevertheless, if economic progress is measured by the success in improving the well-being of the broad masses within nations, there is no doubt that continuing rapid population growth in most developing countries is severely limiting opportunities to substantially reduce the extent of poverty.

The interrelationship of population growth and poverty is most obvious in the visibly overcrowded nations of Asia, the Middle East, and parts of Africa and Latin America. The lack of new arable land to bring under cultivation leaves growing legions without any means of engaging in productive activity. An increased prevalence of hunger and malnutrition and high rates of migration to already overcrowded urban slums on the slender chance of locating an urban job are the frequent results.

Even where land scarcity and overcrowding are not already apparent, population growth remains a major impediment to economic progress. Economic growth is meaningful only when measured in per capita terms, and in a nation whose population is expanding at 3 percent annually, a very respectable economic growth rate of 5 percent brings only a 2 percent annual increase in the production of goods and services per person. The time it takes to double per capita production is lengthened from 14 to 35 years.

Even more harmful to growth prospects is the age structure associated with high population growth rates (see Table 12). When over 40 percent of the population is under age 15, as it is in a majority of the world's nations today, a major portion of national income is necessarily devoted to the struggle to provide basic social services— housing, food, schools, and health services—to this group of dependents. Precious capital and talent must be used to meet elementary human needs for a vast economically unproductive group, rather than to finance the productive investment which could permit more rapid sustained economic growth and thus break the cycle of poverty. And all too often the ability of societies to meet these human needs is simply overwhelmed by the accelerating numbers of people.

Unfortunately, poverty is not an economic abstraction. It is a human condition. It is despair, grief, and pain. It is the despair of a father of seven in a poor country who must join the swelling ranks of unemployed with no prospect of unemployment compensation. Poverty is the longing of a young boy playing outside a village school but unable to enter because his parents lack the few dollars needed to buy textbooks. Poverty is the grief of parents watching helplessly as their three-year-old child dies of a routine childhood disease because, like half of mankind, they do not have access to any medical care.

Table 12. Percentage of Population below Age Fifteen, 1972
(twenty most populous nations)

China	36
India	42
USSR	29
United States	27
Indonesia	45
Japan	24
Brazil	42
Bangladesh	45
Pakistan	44
West Germany	23
Nigeria	45
United Kingdom	24
Italy	24
Mexico	48
France	25
Philippines	43
Thailand	46
Turkey	42
Egypt	42
Spain	28

SOURCE: U.S. Agency for International Development.

The Persistence of Hunger

In the late twentieth century, an era of unprecedented affluence, hunger is still the common lot of much of humanity. For this hungry group, the quality of life is influenced more by the lack of food than by any other single factor. For them, daily existence is circumscribed by the quest for food, reducing life to very fundamental biological terms.

Few of man's needs have resisted fulfillment so strenuously as has the need for food. In countries containing one-third or more of the world's people, average food intake is today below the minimum required for normal growth and activity. Much of the population in these countries suffers from chronic protein malnutrition as well. In those areas where death certificates are issued for pre-school infants in the poor countries, death is generally attributed to measles, pneumonia, dysentery, or some other disease, when in fact these children are more often victims of malnutrition. Severely malnourished infants are children with low resistance, who frequently die of routine childhood diseases. If all the deaths that would not have occurred if the patient had been given adequate nutrition could be attributed to their basic cause with reasonable accuracy, it would bring the social costs of malnutrition into much sharper focus.

The Food and Agriculture Organization has labeled malnutrition "the biggest contributor to child mortality in the developing countries." The World Bank reports that studies in Latin America "show malnutrition to be either the primary cause of—or a major contributing factor in—50 to 75 percent of the deaths of one- to four-year-olds."

Malnutrition has economic as well as social costs. Low food intake has a direct and measurable effect on, for example, the productivity of labor. Construction firms from the industrial countries operating in developing countries and employing local labor often find they get high returns in worker output by investing in a good company cafeteria that serves employees three meals a day.

The impact of nutrition on physical development is unchallenged. The youth of Japan today are visible examples of the change that improved nutrition can bring. Well-nourished as a result of Japan's newly acquired affluence, teen-agers on the streets of Tokyo are on the average perhaps two inches taller than their elders.

Protein is as crucial for children's mental development as for their physical development. This was strikingly shown in a recent study conducted over several years in Mexico; youngsters who had been severely undernourished before the age of five were found to average 13 points lower in I.Q. than a carefully selected control group that had not experienced severe malnutrition. Protein shortages in the early years of life impair development of the brain and central nervous system, permanently reducing learning capacity. Furthermore, this damage is irreversible. If widespread protein shortages are allowed to continue, we risk a loss which no amount of investment in education will correct. In sum, the nutritional deficits of today are depreciating the human resources of tomorrow, preventing many of us from reaching our full humanity.

The role of population growth in perpetuating hunger in the developing nations is brought out clearly in Figures 5 and 6. Food production in the developing world has grown dramatically since the early 1960s, increasing by one-third. Yet by 1973, after a record harvest worldwide, food production *per capita* in the poor nations was a slim 2 percent higher than it was in the early 1960s. Under such conditions, it is extremely difficult to reduce the numbers of the hungry and malnourished, a group that may include one-third of all mankind.

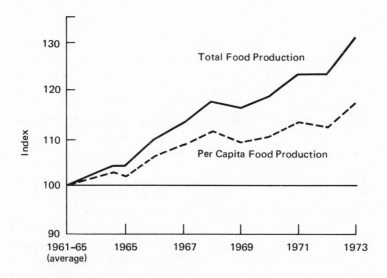

Figure 5
More Developed Countries: Total and Per Capita
Food Production Rises Substantially

Source: U.S. Dept. of Agriculture

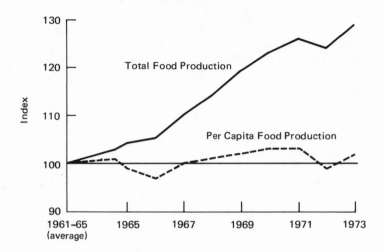

Figure 6
Less Developed Countries*: Population Growth Absorbs
Food Production Increases
*Excluding Communist Asia

Source: U.S. Dept. of Agriculture

Illiteracy: Five Centuries after the Printing Press

Five centuries have passed since the invention of the printing press, yet as of 1970 two-fifths of the world's adults lacked the capacity to take advantage of this basic invention. The United Nations Educational, Scientific and Cultural Organization (UNESCO) estimates that the illiteracy of the world's adult population declined from 43 percent in 1960 to 39 percent in 1965. Although the share of the population affected is thus diminishing slowly, the number of illiterates is greater today than twenty years ago because of growth in population. The modern world is very much a world of words and, despite the new opportunities for learning made possible through radio and television, the illiterate person is severely handicapped.

Adult illiteracy is concentrated largely in Asia, Africa, and Latin America, while illiteracy within the rich countries today is negligible. At least half, and in some cases three-fourths or more, of the adults in many poor societies are illiterate. Compulsory elementary education will eventually eliminate illiteracy, but several decades are required. Unfortunately, mankind may not be able to afford this delay.

Many well-intentioned poor countries, overwhelmed with the vast numbers of children of school age, are finding it impossible to keep up in the provision of schools and teachers. Those countries with the least to spend on education are also those with the highest birth rates. Not only are funds in short supply, but the pyramidal distribution of age groups in a rapidly growing population often results in a decreasing ratio of trained teachers to schoolchildren. The school age population is simply growing more rapidly than schools can be built and teachers trained and recruited within the educational budgets available. As a result, many governments once committed to universal education have quietly abandoned this objective for the foreseeable future.

For modern society, knowledge and information have become the central economic resource, while for the 700 million or so adults who are illiterate, the most basic tools for learning are still lacking. How are they to understand the accelerating pace of change, the consequences of the growing pressures of human activity on the ecosystem, and the technological advances weaving all of mankind into a single community?

People without Jobs

In social terms, perhaps the most disturbing per capita decline among the world's natural resources is in arable land. As population has continued to grow rapidly in the densely populated poor countries with little new land to bring under the plow, the area of arable land per person has shrunk steadily over the past two decades. In parts of Asia, the Middle East, North Africa, East Africa, Central America, and the Andean countries, this decline has reached the point where the cultivable area per person is often not sufficient to permit a person to earn a living with available technologies. Plots of land divided and subdivided over the generations cannot be divided any further. For many young people, there is no means of earning a living in the rural communities where they are born and reared. This is a unique situation in historical terms; for this group there is no longer a place in the countryside, no job waiting in the city, and no new world to which they can emigrate. In short, there is no meaningful economic role in society as currently organized. In economic terms, these are marginal men.

The continually growing number of people without jobs is a phenomenon which promises to become one of the world's gravest social ills during the final quarter of the twentieth century. In many developing countries, entrants into the job market outnumber new jobs being created by two to one, creating levels of unemployment and underemployment far in excess of any the rich countries have ever experienced. The unemployment situation—like the environmental crisis, the widening gap between rich countries and poor ones, and the swelling flow of migrants into the cities—is likely to get much worse before it gets better.

Employment and employment-related issues are likely to dominate international development in the years ahead. The population explosion which began in many poor countries at least fifteen or twenty years ago resulted in an almost immediate demand for food; but since babies do not require jobs, there was a grace period of fifteen or twenty years in the employment situation that did not exist for food. As we enter the mid-1970s, we are approaching the end of this grace period. With the number of young people entering the job market swelling year by year, the day of reckoning with the impact of the population explosion on employment is at hand.

In some poor countries, the labor force is now growing at three times the rate of the industrialized countries (see Table 13). As a result, the number of potentially productive but unemployed people is rising. Within Latin America, the number of unemployed climbed from 2.9 million in 1950 to 8.8 million in 1965, tripling in fifteen years. The visible unemployment rate went from under 6 percent to over 11 percent during this period. Although more recent data on continent-wide unemployment are not available, such national data as are available indicate that the ranks of the unemployed are continuing to swell, and at an alarming rate.

Adding to an already dismal prospect, the classical definition of unemployment—those seeking work at the prevailing wage rates—greatly understates the extent of unemployment because it does not measure the hidden unemployment or underemployment. According to Eric Thorbecke, who has examined the employment situation in Latin America in considerable detail, "If one considers unemployment as the ratio of available but unused labor hours to the total available labor hours, which is one way of measuring both unemployment and underemployment, the magnitude and the seriousness of the problem is magnified. For one continent, Latin America, this technique revealed unemployment equivalent rates ranging from 20 percent in some countries to over 50 percent in others. For the region as a whole it was 26 percent. This was based on data for 1960." If the same data were available for 1970, they would undoubtedly show an unemployment equivalent much higher.

Looking at the developing nations as a whole, the International Labor Office (ILO) estimates that 24.7 percent of the total labor force was either unemployed or underemployed in 1970. The comparable figure for 1980 is expected to rise to 29.5 percent.

In Colombia, one of the few poor countries where the employment situation has been examined in some detail, there is now confirmation that the outlook is bleak. A five-hundred-page report by the ILO describes the situation as follows: "At a conservative estimate one-half million Colombians, out of an active urban labor force of some three million, are seeking work, but are unable to find it. Probably as many again would like to work, but are not currently looking for it, having given up in frustration or having not even started to look with any seriousness, deterred by the knowledge that their chance of finding a job is slim."

The level of unemployment in India began to rise during the 1950s, when it increased from an estimated 11 percent of the labor force in 1951 to 15 percent in 1961. This trend continued during the 1960s as the number of new entrants greatly outstripped the capacity of the economy to create meaningful employment. During the 1970s, India's labor force is projected to increase from 210 million to 273 million, an increment of 63 million. Already plagued with widespread unemployment and underemployment, India is now confronted with 100,000 entrants into the labor force *each week*. One Asian economist, Harry T. Oshima, estimates that 15 percent or more of the labor force is unemployed in Pakistan, Bangladesh, Ceylon, Malaysia, the Philippines, and probably Indonesia.

Among the most alarming socio-economic projections to the end of the century are those of growth in the labor force by the ILO (Table 13). Between 1970 and the end of the century, the labor force in the less developed region is projected to expand by 91 percent, nearly doubling within a one-generation span. Projected labor force growth for the more developed regions during this period is 33 percent.

The ILO sees agricultural employment in the less developed regions expanding only 26 percent during this period. The great bulk of the growth in labor force must be absorbed by the non-agricultural sector, requiring it to expand by 219 percent, more than tripling its current number of jobs. The need to create such a vast increase in such a short period of time calls into question the adequacy and appropriateness of existing national development strategies. It will not be possible to provide jobs on the scale required without a much larger emphasis on

rural development and a labor intensive agricultural development
strategy.

From Countryside to City

The continuous and swelling flow of people from countryside to city
in the poor countries is creating a serious social crisis, the ramifications of which will eventually affect the quality of life among much
of mankind. The returns from the 1970 world census documented
what already seemed obvious, namely, that populations in the poor
countries are converging on the cities at a record pace.

Throughout most of history, people have migrated from countryside to city largely in response to opportunities in the city. Urbanization served as an index of modernization. Today, urbanization in the
poor countries results much more from uncontrolled population
growth and declining opportunities in overpopulated rural areas. Urban pull has been replaced by rural push. Increasingly, urbanization
is serving as an index of frustration and as an indicator of the potential
explosiveness of the urban slums (*bustees* in India, *favellas* in Brazil,
or *gecekondu* in Turkey) being created.

Urbanization as a process is proceeding much more rapidly in the
poor countries than in those which industrialized earlier. Many populations or urban centers in Asia, Africa, and Latin America are growing at 5 to 8 percent yearly, almost regardless of the existing degree
of urbanization. Those with growth rates of 5 percent double in size

Table 13. Projected Growth in World Labor Force, 1970–2000

	1970	1980	1990	2000	Change 1970–2000
		(millions)			(percent)
More developed regions					
Economically active					
population—Total	488	542	592	649	+33
In agriculture	101	75	49	22	−88
Other	387	467	543	627	+62
Less developed regions					
Economically active					
population—Total	1,011	1,239	1,547	1,933	+91
In agriculture	669	725	786	842	+26
Other	342	514	761	1,091	+219

SOURCE: International Labor Office.

in 15 years; those growing 8 percent yearly double in 9 years and quadruple in 18 years.

It now appears likely that the twentieth century will be the one in which human society is transformed from a primarily rural one to one which is primarily urban. Urban populations in the poor countries now totaling 600 million may quadruple over the next three decades. Since urban service facilities are already overburdened, one can conclude that, in the absence of massive external assistance, the level of services will deteriorate in principal urban centers. The human habitat is being transformed from one in which man is close to nature to one which is primarily man-made, where most of mankind lives in intimate association with a vast number of other human beings.

Urbanization in the poor countries has certain distinctive features. One is the rate of transformation. Urban centers in Turkey and Ghana, growing at 7 percent yearly, are representative. Total populations in those countries are doubling every 25 years or so. The population of many large cities in the poor countries is doubling every 10 to 15 years, but that of the urban slums or shantytowns is doubling in many cases in 5 to 7 years.

The population of urban squatters in the Philippines is growing at 12 percent yearly. The population of Calcutta is projected by some to reach 40 to 50 million by the turn of the century. Projections for Lima indicate a population of 6 million by 1990, three-fourths of which will be in what were originally squatter settlements.

Runaway urbanization is resulting in congested living conditions, with the great bulk of rural migrants to the cities ending up in squatter

Table 14. Growth of Selected Cities
in Developing Countries, 1960–70

CITY	ANNUAL GROWTH RATE (per cent)	YEARS TO DOUBLE
Nairobi	6	12
Abidjan	11	6
Accra	7	10
Djakarta	5	14
Bangkok	6	12
Karachi	6	12
São Paulo	6	12
Bogotá	7	10
Mexico City	5	14

SOURCE: World Bank, *Urbanization: Sector Working Paper,* 1971.

communities or shantytowns. The United Nations reports that the sheer magnitude of uncontrolled settlement is revealed in Mexico City, where *colonias proletarias* amount to one-third of the capital's population of 4.5 million, and in Ankara's *gecekondu* ("builders of the night"), where one-half of its 1.5 million people live. As the rate of growth in squatter settlements continues to exceed that of the city proper in most metropolitan areas in the less developed world, often growing at twice the rate of the city itself, we face the prospect that much of mankind will be living in slums and shantytowns by the end of the century. Where one-third to one-half of a city's inhabitants live in the shantytowns ringing the cities, as in several Latin American capitals, municipal and social services (including health, education, and welfare) are drastically overburdened and unable to cope. One can conclude that any increment in urban population will lead to a further deterioration in the quality of urban life as the gap between services available and those needed widens rapidly.

Perhaps more significant than the actual rate of rural-urban migration is the social situation it is creating. The result of the people piling up in the cities, spontaneously and unplanned, is that many of the basic amenities of life are lacking. According to Charles Abrams, "Armies of squatters are taking over every vacant place, not only on the outskirts but even in the centers of towns, and putting up shacks of tin, wood or cardboard. Most of the squatter camps have no services, no schools, no sewers, not even water, except what the squatters fetch in pails or oil drums, or buy at high cost from peddlers. Garbage piles up around their shacks."

The disproportionate need for social services because of rapid urbanization leads to many dangerous situations, particularly in sanitation. Calcutta, for example, has two water systems: one which distributes an intermittent and inadequate supply of filtered water, and the other a continuous supply of unfiltered water at hydrants. The latter is the primary source of water for the cooking, drinking, bathing, and laundering of the vast numbers of street dwellers. Under such conditions, the potential for epidemics of water-borne disease is high. Contagious disease spreads under crowded conditions, and the stifling atmosphere within dwellings leads to a high incidence of tuberculosis. These migrants from destitute, overcrowded rural areas are bearing the cost of society's failure to control human fertility.

While the need for improved and expanded services increases, the indigenous resources for providing them do not. Local tax scales may be adjusted to take more from those in the higher income brackets, but little in additional funds can be squeezed from people who are already unemployed or underemployed. It can even be argued that expanded services may have a negative effect, since they may simply attract even more migrants to the city. Even where urban services are inadequate and not readily accessible to the new migrants, the fact that they exist at all, and are lacking entirely in rural areas, acts as a magnetic force pulling the young to the cities.

Aside from the problem of sheer numbers in relation to resources and amenities, these rural migrants do not adjust readily to the urban social and economic system and milieu. Unprepared for urban living, they tend to remain villagers in an urban setting. The rate at which the migrants make the transition from shantytowns to the city proper and the rate at which shantytowns are upgraded are very slow, only a trickle relative to the incoming flood.

There is little in past human experience against which to assess the social repercussions of the massive rural-urban migration now under way in the poor countries. Alienation and despair are pervasive. The lack of steady employment for the great bulk of the shantytown dwellers is having a deep psychological impact. The combination of the size of this group and its exposure to better living conditions elsewhere within the same city are creating a social tinderbox.

9

The Human Condition
and Population Growth[1]

The detrimental impact of population growth on economic and social progress is rather widely understood. What is not so commonly understood is the impact of social conditions on fertility levels. As the need to slow population growth acquires a new urgency, the conditions under which fertility levels begin falling are being more carefully examined. The historical record indicates that birth rates do not decline very far unless certain social needs are satisfied. Birth rates do not usually decline voluntarily in the absence of an assured food supply, literacy, and at least rudimentary health services.

Given the relationship between social conditions and declining fertility, the challenge for development planners is how to design development strategies which most quickly satisfy the requisite social needs. The effect on fertility of a development strategy for a particular sector, with a given level of resources, can vary widely depending on the nature of the strategy. A strategy designed to distribute the benefits of investment in health, education, and job creation broadly throughout the population will reduce fertility far more than one which concentrates the benefits in a narrow elite group.

[1]Much of the material in this chapter is drawn from the work of two colleagues at the Overseas Development Council: an ODC Monograph, *Smaller Families through Social and Economic Progress,* by William Rich, and a Development Paper, *Growth from Below: A People-Oriented Development Strategy,* by James P. Grant. Both go into these issues in much more detail.

Socio-economic Progress and Fertility

Demographers have long known that with sufficient economic progress, as in Europe and North America, high birth rates fall sharply.
Demographers also have generally recognized that widespread poverty tends to sustain high birth rates for the obvious reason that
families living without adequate employment, education, or health
care have little security for the future except for reliance on their
children. Despite the major reduction in death rates in the past two
decades, many persons in poor countries still perceive—often rightly
so—that having numerous children is advantageous, both for immediate social and economic reasons and because of the persisting risk that
offspring will not survive to adulthood. These high birth rates, in turn,
merely make social problems worse.

The crucial question, therefore, is how the great majority of families
can break out of this vicious circle. Recognizing the fact that their
social and economic difficulties worsen every day that population
growth continues unrestrained, many developing countries have
begun family planning programs to improve means of limiting family
size. But a troublesome problem remains: these programs have for the
most part been accepted by families which are relatively affluent or
already have too many children, or by women in ill health. Unless
there is greater acceptance of the need for fewer children by the
majority of families, efforts to stabilize population growth will fail.
Therefore, if developing countries are to escape the threats posed by
rapid population growth, more families must now not only be provided with means to limit births but also acquire the motivation to do
so.

The experience of Europe and North America during the past
century—a general reduction in birth rates after incomes became
relatively high—was long thought to be the norm, in the absence of
family planning programs, for poor countries as well. However, there
is now striking evidence that in an increasing number of poor countries, as well as in some regions within countries, birth rates have
dropped sharply despite relatively low per capita income and despite
the absence or relative newness of family planning programs. Examination of societies as different as China, Barbados, Sri Lanka, Uruguay, Taiwan, the Indian Punjab, Cuba, and South Korea suggests a
common factor.

In all of these countries, a large portion of the population has gained access to modern social and economic services—such as education, health, employment, and credit systems—to a far greater degree than in most poor countries or in most Western countries during their comparable periods of development. Not only have birth rates dropped noticeably in most of these countries even before the introduction of major family planning programs, but such programs seem to be much more successful in those countries which have assigned high priority in their development programs to a more equitable distribution of income and social services.

The relationship between socio-economic change and fertility is admittedly complex and not reducible to a simple formula. In every country there are variations in cultural or religious factors which have some implications for population growth. Additional variations are due to the means available for reducing births. Yet there is increasing evidence that the very strategies which cause the greatest improvements in the welfare of the entire population also have the greatest effect on reducing population growth.

Education and Fertility

An examination of the relationship between female education and fertility in several societies, both more and less developed, shows a very strong relationship between educational levels and fertility levels. As education levels rise, fertility levels fall. In a number of societies, the attainment of literacy brings with it a sharp decline in fertility. Several studies show that as women acquire literacy they reduce their number of children by about 1.5, or roughly one-third. Studies in other societies, such as Chile, have shown the sharp drop in fertility coming after completion of elementary school (see Table 15). Evidence from Ghana showed the biggest drop in fertility coming with completion of secondary school. Those with university degrees in Ghana had only 0.5 children each, a fertility level well below the average in any more developed country.

Several explanations have been offered of the role of education in reducing the size of families. Education can affect the norms and values of persons in such a way that they begin to question traditional practices of their parents or other authority figures. Persons who go to school or who are literate tend to be more receptive to innovations and have a greater opportunity to come into contact with "change agents" such as health planners or family planning counselors. Extended education is likely to delay marriage and to suggest vocational

Table 15. *Relationship between Educational and Fertility Levels in Ghana, Jordan, and Chile*

EDUCATIONAL LEVEL	NUMBER OF CHILDREN PER WOMAN		
	Ghana	Jordan	Chile
No education	5.7	8.7	4.9
Elementary education	5.2	7.3	1.3
Secondary education	2.5	4.5	1.7
At least one university degree	0.5	4.0	n.a.

SOURCES: C. Miro and W. Mertens, "Influences Affecting Fertility in Urban and Rural Latin America," *Milbank Memorial Fund Quarterly,* July 1968; H. Rizk, "National Fertility Sample Survey for Jordan, 1972: The Study and Some Findings," *Population Bulletin of United Nations Economic and Social Office in Beirut,* July 1973; and UN economic and Social Council, quoted in *People,* October 1973, p. 27.

alternatives to childbearing. Higher educational levels may also be associated with increased economic security, which in turn often means smaller families. All of these explanations help to account for the particularly strong correlation observed between the level of female education and family size.

Educational strategies for developing countries have received growing attention recently from both researchers and policy-makers, but sharp differences of opinion continue on appropriate policy approaches. Problems and failures in many countries reinforce the need for fresh ideas in the field, for new strategies that break away from traditional Western patterns.

One of the dilemmas is that a universal education system can quickly absorb the financial resources and administrative talents of even a reasonably prosperous government, while a system that opens educational opportunities to only a small minority can rapidly institutionalize a strongly hierarchical social relationship. If efforts are made to spread a traditional form of education oriented to urban needs over a wide area, the quality of education in the rural areas is likely to become so irrelevant to the society's need for skills that the entire effort can become socially disruptive. In many poor countries, those who have attained a high level of education find that no appropriate jobs are available to them. Those with sophisticated medical or scientific training often migrate to Europe or the United States (where there are now some 30,000 doctors from the developing countries), in response to lucrative job offers. At the same time, the majority of the population remains deprived of even elementary levels of education as well as the medical and technical services of the professionals who have left the country. This situation clearly results in rising frustration among those who continue to lack minimum educational skills.

The national educational strategies of the developing countries vary widely in terms of the share of the population they are designed to reach. Differences between countries in the distribution of expenditures by level of education are illustrative. The extensive use of public funds in South Korea, for example, to subsidize primary education makes the educational system accessible to a much broader segment of the population than in Brazil, where the lion's share of the educational budget is devoted to subsidizing university education. In 1970, according to government sources in the two countries, two-thirds of the Korean population between the ages of 5 and 14 was in primary school, while only one-half of the same age group was in school in Brazil, despite the higher level of average per capita income in Brazil. In general, strategies focusing on the use of government funds for widespread primary education are likely to affect fertility far more than those which emphasize higher education for a smaller segment of the population.

Health Services and Fertility

There are two indicators which provide insight into the state of health in a society: infant mortality and life expectancy. The two are of course not unrelated. Both correlate quite closely with fertility levels. As infant mortality rates decline, so do birth rates shortly thereafter. As life expectancy increases, birth rates decline. The provision of basic health services to a population is a prerequisite to a rapid drop in population growth.

This relationship may appear somewhat paradoxical, since if the birth rate were to remain the same, a reduction in a society's death rate would, of necessity, result in more rapid population increase. Indeed, the postwar population explosion in most developing nations can be attributed to the initial lowering of death rates below historic levels following the introduction of Western medicine, without a simultaneous reduction in traditionally high birth rates.

However, in those developing nations where birth rates have declined substantially, infant mortality is considerably lower, and life expectancy much longer, than in the less developed world as a whole. The evidence suggests that the improvement of health conditions beyond a certain minimal level is closely associated with a falling birth rate.

Parents generally wish to ensure the survival of at least one son to care for them in old age and to continue the family name. Often, a woman must bear six or more children in order to be certain that one son will survive to adulthood. A Harvard University study conducted under the leadership of David Heer has emphasized how important the assurance of high rates of survival is to the motivation for smaller families. Where mortality rates are very high, parents often have as many children as possible. Where death rates are relatively low and life expectancy 50 years or more, however, each additional reduction in the death rate leads to a far greater reduction in the birth rate, thus resulting in slower over-all population growth.

Not only do infant mortality and life expectancy correlate closely with fertility, but the relationships are rather linear in nature. Cross-sectional data for the world's twenty-five most populous countries show a few countries with infant mortality rates (deaths per thousand in the first year of life) as high as 180. Crude birth rates in these countries are about 50 per thousand. There are several countries in the group which have infant mortality rates of 20 or less. In these countries, birth rates average about 17. Moving from those nations with the highest infant mortality to those with the lowest, for every decline of five in the infant mortality rate, the birth rate drops one.

A similar situation exists for life expectancy. In those countries where life expectancy is among the lowest in the world, about 40 years, birth rates are among the highest, again averaging around 50. There are several countries where life expectancy is now 70 years or more. In this group of countries, birth rates average 17. An examination of cross-sectional data for the twenty-five most populous countries shows that for each increase in life expectancy of one year, birth rates drop by one.

The basic problem in delivering health care is to determine how to improve the health of as much of the population as possible with limited resources. Alternative strategies result in varying levels of training and support of physicians, nurses, midwives, and other paramedical workers and pharmacists as well as in varying levels of capital investment in hospitals, clinics, mobile health units, and other facilities. The usual approach thus far has been to focus on training highly skilled medical doctors and building hospitals—two central components of the Western health system. The effect of this approach in countries where financial resources are scarce has been to provide high-quality health care for a small urban elite, while depriving most of the population of health services altogether.

Experience in several countries illustrates more appropriate strategies. Sri Lanka, for instance, has made a concerted effort over the past two decades to improve health facilities by training large numbers of paramedical workers while maintaining a relatively small core of fully trained doctors. Thus, although the level of health expenditures per person remains quite low, life expectancy has increased from 54 to 62 years over the same period. These results provide a marked contrast to the situation in some other countries with a similar per capita governmental expenditure for health care.

An examination of the health care delivery system of South Korea further underlines weaknesses in the approach of many countries. While the number of doctors, dentists, and midwives per thousand people in South Korea is not too different from that in other countries, the number of pharmacists may be several times greater. Access to health services in rural areas is far superior in the case of Korea. The pronounced edge in low-cost medical treatment in Sri Lanka and Korea yields a life expectancy of several additional years and infant mortality rates of 50 and 53 per thousand, respectively, less than half that of many other countries with a comparable income level.

Perhaps the most dramatic improvements in health care in the last two decades have occurred in China. Inheriting a seriously inadequate health care system, the government gaining power in 1949 placed high priority on improvements in this field. Initial steps were taken to improve environment, sanitation, and personal hygiene. Major pests were exterminated and millions of persons were vaccinated. During the mid-1960s, doctors were sent out to rural areas, and mobile medical teams were assigned to service remote areas of the country. Major emphasis was placed on the education of paramedical personnel. In many cases people were recruited from the countryside, trained in nearby medical centers, and then returned to their villages. Most recently, China has instituted a system of "barefoot doctors," trained to provide first aid, give inoculations, and carry out simple health procedures—including the performance of abortions and the distribution of contraceptives. Cases that are too complicated for these "barefoot doctors" are referred to fully trained doctors who have been located throughout the country.

Unfortunately, many governments have devoted a large portion of their total investment in health services to the construction of a few modern hospitals in urban areas, while the needs of the rural population were largely ignored. A new, modern hospital may be accessible to only a small and relatively privileged portion of the population; a similar level of investment in rural clinics and dispensaries and the training of paramedics might reach far more people. Until the minimal base of medical aid is available to a large majority of the population, the costs and benefits of hospital construction might better be calculated in terms of lives lost because of failure in the distribution of health services.

Food and Fertility

An assured food supply plays an important role in reducing birth rates. When malnutrition is widespread, even common childhood diseases are often fatal. The relationship between nutrition and human fertility is summed up in the observation that good nutrition is the best contraceptive. It is no coincidence that virtually all well-fed societies have low fertility, and poorly fed societies have high fertility. The effect of nutrition on fertility is in large measure indirect, through its effect on the infant mortality rate and on over-all life expectancy. Where malnutrition is widespread, it is virtually impossible to achieve low infant mortality rates.

Adequate nutrition in terms of both calories and protein is usually achieved when annual per capita grain availability reaches about 550 pounds, assuming reasonably equitable distribution within the country. Of the twenty-five most populous countries, eight have per capita grain availability above 700 pounds per year. All have crude birth rates below 20.

The state of nutrition in the world at any given time is a result of the amount of food produced, how it is distributed both within and among societies, and how efficiently agricultural commodities are used. If a large share of the world's supply of cereals is converted into meat, milk, and eggs, providing excessively high protein intake levels in some societies, people elsewhere in the world may not have enough cereals to meet even basic caloric needs, much less critical protein needs.

Within individual developing countries, agricultural sector development strategies are important both because they affect the quantity and quality of food available and because they affect the distribution of employment and the benefits of agricultural development. Rural development efforts around the world reflect a wide range of decisions regarding the selection of the technologies, landownership policies, terms of credit, and other measures that are likely to influence the distribution of the benefits of agricultural progress.

Where unemployment and underemployment are rampant, as in many developing nations, a strategy combining extensive land tenure reform, credit, marketing, and other services with the introduction of improved crop varieties can both provide more jobs and expand production. Owners of small farms and landless laborers who were formerly underemployed can—if seeds, fertilizer, and tube wells or their equivalent for irrigation are made available—carry on intensive production on relatively small plots of land. Such reform permits unemployed and underemployed laborers to be more productively utilized —thus both expanding the national product and improving the distribution of income, by making certain that those at the relatively low end of the pay scale will be the ones to benefit most.

Alternative agricultural development strategies may be successful in increasing production but have vastly different social effects on birth rates. Both Taiwan and Mexico, for example, have enjoyed the benefits of the Green Revolution. In Mexico, however, improved wheat harvests have contributed relatively little to alleviating rural poverty. In 1960, over half of Mexico's total agricultural output was produced on only 3 percent of its farms. This same 3 percent accounted for 80 percent of the increase in agricultural production between 1950 and 1960. Owners of large-scale, capital intensive, irrigated farms were by far the largest beneficiaries of the new wheats. In a ten-year period, the number of landless laborers increased 43 percent, while the average number of days worked each year dropped from 194 to 100.

In Taiwan, on the other hand, the emphasis has been on enabling small farmers to participate in the development process as a consequence of a strictly enforced 7.5-acre limit on individual landholdings. The average farm of about 2.2 acres is owned by the tiller. By virtue of an excellent system of farm cooperatives and widely available educational and low-cost health facilities, the average farmer has access to credit, markets, new technology, health services, and education to a degree usually available in most countries only to far more affluent farmers. As a result, small-scale rice farmers have been able to take advantage of the new crops; they have almost doubled their output in the past twenty years, while at the same time providing more employment for rural dwellers. Farms in Taiwan now average five times as many workers per 100 acres as those in Mexico, and their output of food grains per acre is nearly treble that of Mexico.

Unemployment and Fertility

Availability of employment is another factor that, at least indirectly, influences the birth rate. For several reasons, full-time employment is often the key to other opportunities for improved welfare. When only marginal employment is available—such as sidewalk vending in the cities or harvest work in rural areas—then families may consider it necessary to have as many children as possible to contribute to family support. On the other hand, if women can find jobs, they are more likely to postpone having children, or decide to have only one or two. Sending children to school instead of to income-producing work can also affect motivation for family size. As child labor practices change, the cost of rearing children increases.

In Western economies, unemployment rates above 6 percent cause political leaders to hit the panic button, but in many poor countries, as noted in the previous chapter, unemployment rates of 15 percent or more are increasingly common. If underemployment is included, the figure may well rise to 30 percent for some countries.

The growing ranks of unemployed are a source of social unrest and potential political disruption. Rising unemployment has been a political issue in elections in India and Chile during the early years of this decade. It is now clear that traditional approaches to development are not very effective in coping with this problem. A rapid rate of economic growth may be necessary but not sufficient to reduce unemployment. Argentine economist Raul Prebisch estimates that Latin America must average a rate of economic growth of at least 8 percent during the 1970s if it is even to hold the line on unemployment.

Unfortunately, Western economic experience does not have much to offer in the way of solutions to this dilemma. Capital intensive technologies originating in the Western industrial nations are becoming less and less relevant to the labor surplus economies of the poor countries. The earlier Japanese experience is more relevant, since Japan did develop under conditions of dense population, cheap labor, scarce capital, and scarce land. An unfortunate result of Japan's defeat in World War II was that it discouraged many developing countries from drawing on certain valuable aspects of Japan's developmental experience.

Policies designed to encourage labor intensive techniques in industrial production are important, but even more crucial are agricultural strategies. Despite the high rate of urban migration, a majority of the population in most developing nations will still be living in rural areas throughout this century. The "efficient" Japanese and the "efficient" Americans have utilized two vastly different approaches to agriculture—with Japan maximizing the use of its (until recently) relatively plentiful labor on scarce land, and with the United States making maximum use of capital and minimum use of scarce labor on its plentiful land. In recent years, the developing countries that have achieved highest per acre productivity and labor intensiveness have been those that have generally followed the Japanese rather than the American or Russian models, which are high on output per man, but result in a underutilization of both scarce land and plentiful labor in many developing countries.

Thus in developing nations that have encouraged labor intensive agriculture, including Egypt, Taiwan, and South Korea, the average number of workers per hundred acres is over 70. In Mexico, Brazil, the Philippines, and India, the same figure ranges from 12 to 36 workers. The intensive use of labor in farming in the former group of nations is one important reason why grain yields per acre are from two to three times higher than in the latter group.

A broad-based agricultural development strategy in turn provides the greatest boost for employment in non-agricultural sectors as well. As income rises among the rural poor, demand escalates rapidly for a variety of simple tools and consumer goods. Often, the desired goods can be produced in rural and small-scale industries that are labor intensive and that tend to require very few imported industrial inputs.

Economic Growth: Necessary but Not Sufficient

There is today a great deal of dissatisfaction with economic development efforts in the poor countries. Disappointment and disillusionment exist not so much because goals of the 1960s were not attained as because the ambitious growth goals set at the beginning of the decade no longer seem adequate. Goals for the first development decade were expressed almost entirely in economic growth terms. The object was to raise the average economic growth rate to 5 percent, permitting modest gains in per capita income.

At the end of the decade it was evident that the single pursuit of growth more often than not resulted in a worsening distribution of income. The general model appeared to be one in which the lower quarter of society suffered a decline in its share of the national economic pie. Indeed, in some situations the economic well-being of this group may even have deteriorated in absolute terms over the past decade.

The detailed ILO study of employment and income distribution trends in Colombia, a country achieving substantial economic growth over the past fifteen years, reports "the bottom one-third of the rural population may be no better off today than in the 1930's." Within Mexico, the income of the upper one-fifth of the population was ten times that of the lower one-fifth in 1950. By 1969, it was sixteen times as great. A similar worsening of income distribution occurred in many other countries for which data are available, such as Sri Lanka and the Philippines.

Addressing this issue involves more than merely adopting a progressive tax policy to redistribute income. Rather, it means designing a development strategy that by its nature distributes the benefits of progress more evenly and that satisfies the basic social needs of the population as a whole as quickly as possible.

A country that distributes goods and services on an equitable basis can bring about improvements in the welfare of the relatively poor on a wide scale even if its total resource availability is low. Thus in Taiwan, average incomes are relatively well distributed, health services have extended throughout rural areas, and effective primary education is accessible to virtually all of the population. In Mexico, although average income is almost double that in Taiwan, the distribution of benefits is more limited, other social services are poorly shared, and the well-being of the poorest groups is extremely low. As a result, the income of the poorest 20 percent of the population is higher in Taiwan than in Mexico, and the "real income"—which would include measures for health and education—is noticeably higher in Taiwan.

Keeping in mind these differences in the distribution of income and services, it is interesting to note that in Taiwan the crude birth rate dropped from 46 per thousand in 1952 to 31 in 1963, when a vigorous family planning program was introduced. It continued falling thereafter to 24 in 1972. In Mexico, on the other hand, the birth rate only declined from 44 to 43 during the period 1952–72. While the birth rate is declining for a few areas of greatest progress, this trend has not yet affected the majority of the Mexican population.

In South Korea, as a result of socio-economic improvements, the crude birth rate dropped from 45 in 1958 to 38 in 1964, by which time a family planning program had been implemented. The birth rate continued to fall to about 29 in 1972, which reduced the population growth rate to approximately 2 percent. In Brazil, on the other hand, the birth rate only declined from about 42 to 37 during the period 1958–72. As in Mexico, this trend has not affected the majority of the population. Highly uneven distribution of income and social services, religious constraints, and a lack of government support for family planning programs have all contributed to the maintenance of Brazil's high population growth rate.

The experience of recent years also indicates quite clearly that these more equitable approaches to development, which are so beneficial in increasing the motivation for smaller families, need not be at the expense of economic growth. In fact, those development strategies that provide social justice through making it possible for a farmer or a laborer to work more effectively for his own advancement can actually accelerate growth. Even though this conclusion runs counter to much past economic thinking, it should not be too surprising. If 20 percent of a poor country's rural labor force is idle, a labor intensive agricultural strategy putting the unemployed to work will substantially increase over-all production; and the provision of basic education and health services to farmers generally should increase production further—as well as improve the motivation for smaller families in the rural sector.

Some objections that have been raised to the idea that improvements in social welfare generally bring lower birth rates should perhaps be noted. The facts that high population growth rates continue most dramatically in Latin America despite the region's relatively high per capita incomes, and that the most successful examples of rapidly declining birth rates in countries with low per capita incomes are in East Asia, have led many to say that Catholicism is the dominant reason for the former and that Chinese cultural attributes are responsible for the latter.

Obviously, religious and cultural factors have some impact on attitudes toward family size; it must not be forgotten, however, that comparable policies and programs have been shown to have roughly comparable effects in different religious and cultural settings. Thus there is a significant correlation between education and fertility in Catholic Chile, just as there is in Africa, Asia, and the Middle East. Similarly, we know that Catholic France has long had low birth rates, and that the relatively more prosperous Catholic north of Yugoslavia has a significantly lower birth rate than Yugoslavia's much poorer Muslim south. With regard to the alleged greater Chinese cultural willingness to shift toward smaller families, it bears remembering that similar improvements in education, health, income, and jobs have apparently had roughly comparable effects among the Sinhalese in Sri Lanka, Indians and Tamals in Singapore, blacks in Barbados, Cubans and Uruguayans in Latin America, and Punjabis in India as they have had on the Chinese in East Asia.

Development Means Reform

In many countries, adopting the policies outlined here requires major changes in the way in which power is exercised. Such changes will not be easy. Established interests in any country naturally resist reforms aimed at removing much of their power. Effective land reform programs require a shift in power from landlord to tenant. Effective low-cost health systems that reach an entire population require changes in doctors' professional attitudes and standards to allow widespread use of less costly, but also less qualified, paramedics. Unions are reluctant to slow their demands for wage increases, where surplus labor is available, as a way of reducing incentives to use labor-saving machinery. Similarly, in both low-income and high-income countries, the phasing out of inefficient industries for the sake of the long-run benefits of freer trade is no easy matter.

We know how difficult such adjustments are to handle in a wealthy, "modern" society like the United States; Americans are still at odds over the "hows" and "whys" of full employment, free trade, and national health care policies. Yet if leaders in developing countries pursue economic growth without reforming existing political, economic, and social structures, the ultimate result will be failure to reach national goals. As the American and European experience of the past century demonstrates, development is not possible without constant change in these structures.

How can these needed changes be brought about? Some—such as more realistic interest and foreign exchange rates, health systems designed to reach the majority and not just the few, changes of government practices in such areas as project design and contracting, and encouragement of credit mechanisms for small producers—are relatively easy to introduce once a determined government understands the issues. Others, such as land tenure reforms, may be much more difficult to achieve.

A sense of crisis is the determining factor in creating a climate for change that forces governments to act: the political costs of inaction must appear to exceed the cost of action. Thus the serious food shortages in South Asia during the mid-1960s partially explain the policy changes then made in India and Pakistan to make possible a Green Revolution; a lack of crisis, on the other hand, helps explain why these changes have yet to be made in most Latin American countries. Thus the major reforms in Singapore, for example, were greatly facilitated by the sense of urgency created by major crises during the past eight years: separation from Malaysia and the loss of the Malaysian market; economic confrontation with Indonesia; and the unexpectedly rapid British withdrawal. In American history, too, the New Deal social reforms were a direct consequence of the Depression.

The present problem in many cases is that the "crisis" of overpopulation often has the appearance of being a concern for the future, and political leaders used to operating in a short time frame may not appreciate the urgent need for acting today to minimize the unavoidable crisis which will appear tomorrow. One need, then, is for leaders to become more aware of and responsible for current policies designed to ameliorate future threats to national welfare. Perhaps even more important is the need for analysts, the media, and leadership to become more aware of the underlying role of population growth in many *current* national problems, ranging from a shortage of domestic savings for investment to unemployment to environmental deterioration. In many cases, present-day national welfare is being threatened by rapid population growth to a much greater degree than is generally realized.

Summary

William Rich summarizes well in his monograph the arguments for an approach to the population problem which goes beyond family planning: "In a number of poor countries, birth rates have dropped sharply despite relatively low per capita income and despite relative newness of family planning programs. The common factor in these countries is that the *majority* of the population has shared in the economic and social benefits of significant national progress to a far greater degree than in most poor countries—or in most Western countries during their comparable periods of development. Appropriate policies for making health, education, and jobs more broadly available to lower income groups in poor countries contribute significantly toward the motivation for smaller families that is the prerequisite of a major reduction in birth rates. Combining policies that give special attention to improving the well-being of the poor majority of the population with large-scale, well-executed family planning programs should make it possible to stabilize population in developing countries much faster than reliance on either approach alone."

If the developing countries are to escape the threat posed by rapid population growth within an acceptable time frame, more families must acquire the *motivation* to limit births, not only be provided with improved *means* to do so. The population crisis must be confronted in the broader context of the development crisis—with more emphasis on the possible ways of treating the basic "disease" of poverty and thereby creating the needed motivation for smaller families.

Needless to say, development planning is becoming a much more complex matter than it appeared to be a decade ago. Encouragingly, the need to distribute income more equitably, to spread employment by emphasizing labor intensive technologies, to achieve higher living levels with a lower resource availability and to raise people above the demographic socio-economic threshold all point to a certain cohesiveness in development planning. And we are learning that contrary to the assumptions of the 1960s, policies that enhance social equity and motivation for smaller families can be so designed that they need not deter, and should even accelerate, over-all economic growth.

Part V *CONFRONTING THE*
POPULATION THREAT

10

Evolution of
Population Policies

In reviewing the world population problem, and particularly in attempting to develop an effective plan of action to cope with it, it is useful to consider the historical evolution of population policies, at both the national and international levels. Population size is not a new concern for national governments. Within the United Nations, a wide variety of governmental and nongovernmental bodies are at present involved in efforts to help nations understand their demographic problems and reduce their birth rates.

The evolution of an activist UN role has not been without stress. For many years, religious opposition, particularly from the predominantly Catholic countries, and political opposition, particularly from the socialist countries, stymied efforts by many UN officials and member nations to provide leadership in this critical problem area. In many ways, the 1960s were a decade of transition. Religious opposition diminished and some of the socialist nations themselves moved to the forefront in providing national family planning programs.

During the first two decades of UN existence, its role was largely limited to data gathering, research, and analysis of demographic problems. It was only with the creation of the United Nations Fund for Population Activities (UNFPA), in 1967, that the UN assumed an activist role and began providing global leadership on population issues. The UNFPA, under the leadership of Rafael Salas, has become a major force in organizing, financing, and coordinating national efforts to slow population growth.

Shortly thereafter the UN designated 1974 as World Population Year. Plans were laid for a World Population Conference, to be held in August 1974 in Bucharest. Former Mexican Foreign Minister Antonio Carillo-Flores was nominated secretary-general of the conference, where a World Plan of Action will be considered.

National Population Policies

Prior to World War II and the evolution of modern weapons with their enormous destructive power, most nations were interested in expanding their populations as a means of increasing their political power and influence. To the extent that nations were interested in population, their interest was almost entirely pronatalist. This was particularly true in Europe, where the nation-state originated. In the New World, population expansion through both natural increase and immigration was encouraged in order to push back frontiers and exploit vast undeveloped resources.

As recently as the period between the first and second world wars, the concern of national governments with population was still primarily that their populations might be declining. Germany, France, Italy, and the Scandinavian countries were among the nations whose policies were designed to raise birth rates during the interwar period.

Only since 1950 has there been much concern at the governmental level with the negative consequences of population growth. Only since 1950 have national governments in either the developed or the less developed countries become involved in the provision of family planning services. One notable exception was the Soviet Union, which began to provide family planning services to its people in 1920, though not within the context of a policy to slow the nation's growth rate. The first developing country to formulate an official population policy and adopt a government-sponsored family planning program was India in 1952.

Over the last decade or so, of course, a growing number of developing countries have formulated policies designed to curb population growth and have organized family planning programs. As of 1972, some fifty-nine developing countries, containing 87 percent of the population of the less developed world, had adopted programs to reduce birth rates. Of this total, 74 percent lived in countries whose governments were committed to the specific objective of slowing population growth, while 13 percent lived in countries where government support of family planning was presented to the public in terms of health improvement or for other reasons. By 1974, those less developed countries which had not yet adopted policies to slow population growth were in a distinct and rapidly dwindling minority.

Population policy directives in some countries refer to the slowing of population growth as a general objective, while others have set very specific goals and timetables. Some governments confine their efforts to the organization of family planning programs. Others take a broad, comprehensive approach utilizing a wide range of economic and social policies to reduce family size.

An understanding of how a wide array of economic and social policies and programs can be used to slow population growth is perhaps best gained by again examining the effort now under way in China. As of the mid-1970s, it may have undertaken the most comprehensive, ambitious effort to reduce births of any major country in the world.

To begin with, the Chinese government has worked hard to satisfy what it determined were the basic social needs of the Chinese people. For a country with limited economic and natural resources, it has been remarkably successful in achieving ambitious goals in mass literacy, nutrition, and public health, and most people are now provided with social security for their old age. At the same time, a nationwide network of family planning clinics has been established, offering the full panoply of free contraceptive services, including the modern ones such as the pill, the IUD, and sterilization as well as condoms. The nationwide availability of family planning services is further reinforced by an intensive educational program designed to instill an awareness of the relationship between China's future population growth and well-being at both the individual and national level. Abortion services are readily available in both urban and rural areas, also free of charge. A recommended minimum age of marriage of 28 years for men and 25 years for women is another aspect of the Chinese effort to reduce birth. Ration cards are reportedly issued for only three children per family, and in some localities possibly only for two children. Government-supported efforts to secure equal rights for women in all spheres of economic and political activity are designed to provide means of self-fulfillment other than childbearing.

In addition to efforts by national governments to create the social conditions conducive to declining fertility and to provide family planning services, there is a lengthening list of governments that are beginning to use social and economic pressures to reduce births. Predominantly Muslim Tunisia limits child allowances to the first four children, has legalized the sale of contraceptives, and has passed legislation establishing equal rights for women. Bangladesh has raised the legal minimum age for marriage. The Philippines recently limited tax deductions for four children and accorded working wives the right to deduct 10 percent of their gross income from their tax base. Singapore has introduced perhaps more "disincentives" to childbearing than any other country: income tax deductions for the first three children only; paid maternity leave for the first two confinements only; a progressive rise in the delivery price for each child after the first; and priority in subsidized housing for couples with two or fewer children.

Other governments have altered policies or repealed legislation that hindered efforts to plan families. Mali, like Tunisia, repealed the legislation inherited from French colonial rule forbidding the sale of contraceptives. Iraq has repealed a range of restrictive laws, making it possible now to import all types of contraceptives duty free.

In the economic sphere, a number of governments are now making family planning programs an integral part of multi-year economic development programs. For example, Indonesia's five year plan for 1971–75 incorporates a target of 6 million acceptors of contraceptive services during the plan period. In Bangladesh's first five year plan, family planning is accorded equal priority with food production. Dorothy Nortman of the Population Council quotes from Sri Lanka's five year plan for 1971–76: "The continuous growth of population at the present high rates will pose problems which would defy every attempt at solution." Even though Sri Lanka has made much more progress in reducing its birth rates than most countries, it is still fearful of the consequences of continuing population growth.

Family Planning Practices: A Global Overview

A recent worldwide survey by the International Planned Parenthood Federation (IPPF) estimated that 31 percent of all couples of fertile age were practicing family planning as of 1971. The percentage varied widely from country to country, ranging from below 20 percent in many societies to above 80 percent in others. Of the 31 percent over-all figure, roughly half relied on traditional techniques, such as withdrawal, the condom, and the rhythm method. The other half relied on more modern techniques, such as the pill, the IUD, and sterilization. Worldwide, the condom was probably the most widely used contraceptive during the 1960s; by the 1970s, it was being replaced by the pill. Data for 1970 and 1971 show the pill and sterilization becoming steadily more important relative to the more traditional techniques and the IUD.

Those countries that had the most effective family planning programs offered a variety of contraceptives. For some individuals, or in some cultural situations, one contraceptive technique might be preferable to another. Those interested in spacing children might prefer the pill, while those prepared to avoid any further childbearing might find sterilization more satisfactory.

One of the significant findings of the IPPF survey was the extent to which abortion was used as a means of limiting births. At the global level, expenditures for abortion apparently exceeded those of all other forms of contraception combined. Terminating a pregnancy through abortion is far more costly in economic terms than avoiding the pregnancy through the use of contraceptive practices. It is, however, effectively used in many countries as a back up to contraceptive practices when they fail, as most do from time to time.

Within individual countries, the techniques for controlling births vary widely. Some countries have built their programs around the use of the IUD and the pill, some rely primarily on the condom, still others rely heavily on abortion. In some countries—for example, Japan and India—the pill has not yet been officially cleared for use. In Japan, the condom is used at one time or another by 68 percent of all married couples, and accounts for most contraception, exceeding all other methods combined. Not infrequently, Japanese couples use the condom in conjunction with the "safe period," with abortion regarded as a socially acceptable last resort in the event of contraceptive failure. The family planning program in India relies heavily on the condom (which is marketed through a commercial network at a subsidized price) and sterilization, principally vasectomy.

A number of more developed Western countries now rely primarily on the use of the pill, the IUD, and sterilization, backed by abortion. In several Eastern European countries and the Soviet Union, abortion is the major means of limiting births, in some cases almost to the exclusion of other contraceptive practices.

Pills, IUDs, and Voluntary Sterilization

Widespread use of the pill, the IUD, and voluntary sterilization of both women and men have emerged as important means of limiting births only since 1960. A study by the Population Council on trends in the use of the pill and the IUD in the United States is perhaps illustrative of acceptance trends of these contraceptive techniques in some other countries as well. Both were introduced on a commercial scale in the early 1960s. Among the sample of married women on which the study was based, the use of the pill increased from zero to 31 percent of the group within eight years, after which its use appeared to plateau, at least temporarily. With the IUD, the rate of increase was much slower but more steady, reaching 7 percent. At the time of the study, there was not yet any indication that the upward trend was leveling off.

One advantage of both the pill and the IUD is that neither is coitus-related, in contrast to more traditional techniques such as condoms and diaphragms. The principal disadvantage of the pill—occasional minor negative side effects—has been partially alleviated by reducing the dosage in women affected. The disadvantage of the IUD is that it often causes bleeding, cramps, and general discomfort. Many women simply cannot tolerate an IUD, while it causes no difficulty at all for others. It is ideal for those who can tolerate its use, since it is inexpensive, easily inserted, and readily reversible.

An economic disadvantage of the pill is that it must be used continuously, requiring an indefinite outlay of funds. However, this requirement for regular use may prove an advantage in the longer run, since it provides an incentive for international pharmaceutical houses to engage in distribution and marketing of the pill, holding out the prospect that they may become a major factor in the global spread of family planning. In countries where officially supported family planning programs either do not exist or have only recently been organized, commercial distribution of contraceptives now accounts for a far larger share of the distribution of contraceptives than official programs. This was true as of 1971 for countries such as Venezuela, Turkey, and Thailand.

Voluntary sterilization has achieved a new importance in efforts to limit births over the past decade or so. It is not a new technology, but its widespread use is relatively new. Sterilization, one of the few birth control techniques that can be employed by both males and females, has become quite popular in two major countries, India and the United States, in the past several years. In India, the emphasis from the beginning has been on the sterilization of males, a relatively simple operation. Within the United States, the inability of some women to tolerate the IUD and concern over possible side effects of the pill led many husbands to consider vasectomies. This led to an upsurge in the number of such operations in the early 1970s, with male sterilizations exceeding female sterilizations for the first time.

Liberalization of Abortion Laws

Among the more traditional techniques commonly employed to prevent births in virtually every society is abortion. While reliable data are not available for most countries, those authorities who are best informed estimate that 40 million unwanted pregnancies are terminated by induced abortions in the world each year. Were these pregnancies not terminated, the current annual increase in world population would be closer to 110 million than 70 million.

The 40 million abortions induced each year, many of them illegal, attest to either an unfulfilled demand for contraceptives, the failure of existing contraceptive techniques, or in some cases a preference for abortion over contraception. In countries where modern contraceptives are not widely available and abortion is readily available, it is not uncommon for the number of abortions to exceed live births. Data for the late 1960s indicate that abortions exceed live births by a substantial margin in both the Soviet Union and Hungary.

A commission appointed by the Indian government to study abortion there reports an estimated 3.8 million induced abortions each year, of which an estimated 180,000 result in maternal death. Survival odds for an American soldier going to Vietnam in 1970 at the height of the Vietnam war were much higher than for a pregnant Indian woman considering an induced abortion. Clearly the willingness to take such grave risks is an index of the desperation among women wishing to prevent unwanted births.

Under proper conditions, the termination of a pregnancy during the early months is a safe procedure, in fact safer than childbirth as such. In those countries with good obstetric services, maternal mortality associated with childbirth averages about 20 for every 100,000 births. In less developed countries, maternal mortality can range as high as 500 per 100,000 births. In countries with good obstetric services, legal abortion in early pregnancy usually results in a maternal death rate of 2 to 4 per 100,000.

Where the desire to limit births precedes the availability of contraceptive services, induced abortions may rise rapidly, reaching near epidemic proportions, as in some Latin American societies today. Widespread resort to induced abortions in localities where professional services are not readily available imposes a heavy burden on health services for "medical salvage" procedures. In some large urban hospitals in Latin America, an estimated quarter of all maternity beds are required to treat post-abortion cases.

In response to these and other factors, there has been a widespread international effort to liberalize the conditions under which abortions are available. Over the past generation, this effort has made considerable progress. As of early 1974, five of the six most populous countries in the world—China, India, the Soviet Union, the United States, and Japan—now permit abortion in early pregnancy. Although the economic and social circumstances in these five countries are quite varied, the end result is essentially the same: giving a woman the right to decide whether or not she wishes to bear a child.

Professor Luke T. Lee of Tufts University, an authority on laws affecting population growth, points out that there are many different roads leading to the legalization of abortion. "Whether it be accomplished through judicial decisions (United States), liberal interpretation of existing laws (Japan), new legislation (India), or party action (mainland China), depends on the unique features of each country's legal system. But the result in these five countries is to confirm the right of a woman or couple and medical adviser to make their own personal or professional judgment. Thus, despite some continuing opposition, the majority of the world's population now has legal access to abortion as a means of fertility control."

As of early 1974, those countries that permit legal abortion on broad grounds, including the mental, social, and economic well-being of the woman concerned, contain 2.3 billion people, or 60 percent of the world's population (see Table 16). The share of the world population now in countries with liberal policies toward abortion is up sharply from a few years ago and is continuing to climb.

The worldwide trend toward liberalization of abortion laws and practices appears to be very clear as the pressures to limit population and to reduce maternal mortality increase. Where contraceptive services are not readily available, abortion, whether legal or not, is playing an increasingly important role. In effect, the worldwide movement toward recognition of a woman's right to abort an unplanned fetus reflects a shifting concern for the quality of life relative to quantity, and the growing determination of women everywhere to gain control of their own bodies and lives.

Scarcely a month passes without progress in some country either to liberalize abortion laws or to interpret existing laws more liberally. Existing laws interfering with individual choice in this matter are being challenged almost everywhere they still prevail. In some countries, the medical profession is taking the leadership; in others, women's groups provide the principal organizing focus. A cross section of society in Belgium, including women, youth, and the medical

Table 16. *Countries with Legal Abortion in 1974*

COUNTRY	1972 POPULATION (millions)
Bulgaria	8.6
China, People's Republic	779.4
Cyprus	.6
Czechoslovakia	14.4
Denmark	5.0
Germany, East	17.0
Finland	4.7
Hungary	10.4
Iceland	.2
India	583.0
Iran	32.8
Japan	105.3
North Vietnam	20.1
Norway	3.9
Poland	32.9
Rumania	20.6
Sierra Leone	2.7
Singapore	2.2
South Korea	32.7
Sweden	8.1
Tunisia	5.3
Uganda	10.2
United Kingdom	55.5
United States	207.3
Uruguay	2.9
USSR	246.3
Yugoslavia	20.6
Zambia	4.6
Total population with legal abortion	2,227.3
Total world population, 1972	3,741.2
Percentage of world population in countries with legal abortion	60%

SOURCE: Transnational Family Research Institute and U.S. Agency for International Development.

profession and comprising both Protestants and Catholics, has organized into the Belgian Society to Liberalize Abortion. Similar groups are springing up in other European countries that have not yet liberalized abortion laws. The issue is not whether abortion should be permitted, since it is permitted in most countries under some circumstances. Almost all countries, for example, permit abortion in the event of rape, incest, a threat to the mother's life from childbirth, or possible transmission of hereditary disease. The objective now is to broaden the conditions under which a woman may legally obtain an abortion in an appropriate medical facility.

For many reasons, few would choose abortion as the ideal means of reducing human fertility. But given the absence of absolutely failure-proof and problem-free contraceptives, the avoidance of unwanted children is possible only if legal, medically safe abortions are available to every woman, regardless of her ability to pay.

11

Growing Awareness of the Population Threat

Since 1960, the global economy has expanded at a record 4 to 5 percent annually. At any other period in history, this would have brought widespread and unquestioned improvements in the quality of life for virtually everyone, but this is no longer the case. While the per capita supply of goods and services produced by man was increasing at a record rate, the supply of resources and amenities provided by nature was declining, also at a record rate.

The global population increase of nearly 700 million during the 1960s was roughly the same as that occurring between 1800 and 1900. This increase of more than 20 percent brought a corresponding decline in per capita natural resources, since the latter are in fixed supply. For each of us, there was nearly one-fifth less fresh water, mineral reserves, arable land, fossil fuel reserves, living space, waste absorptive capacity, marine protein, and natural recreation areas in 1970 than in 1960.

The significance of this dramatic decline in natural amenities, which is continuing at an unabated rate during the 1970s, goes far beyond the mere arithmetic of the decline itself. This changing relationship between man and the finite natural system within which he exists is not merely an ecological phenomenon. It has profound economic, political, and social consequences which we are only beginning to perceive.

Declining Options

One senses today a situation in which population growth is beginning, in various ways, to affect our life styles, reducing the options open to the individual. Having said this, however, it is difficult to articulate and document the ways in which this is occurring, in part because so little empirical research has been undertaken in this area. In large measure, the field is a conceptual vacuum. Nonetheless, the following pages do suggest some ways in which individual choices are being restricted by population-induced pressures.

As we press closer to the earth's resource limits, we find the need to regulate human activity increasing exponentially. Population growth is beginning to counter the effect of economic development which, by definition, seeks to increase the options available to the individual. These options involve the activities that make up our daily lives, including what we eat, where we live, and where we travel.

As economic development progresses, our diets become more varied. The most general trend, which seems to be common to all societies as development occurs, is from a diet heavily dependent on a few starchy staples to one greatly enriched with high-protein livestock products. This trend may be arrested by the growing pressure of population on the world's food resources. In some instances, nations are already experiencing at least a temporary downturn in per capita intake of livestock products. Within Argentina, per capita consumption of beef has declined from nearly 200 pounds to less than 140 pounds in recent years. A comparable percentage decline has occurred in the United Kingdom's beef consumption. A principal reason for the pronounced trend in Britain toward substituting poultry products for beef is that poultry is both less expensive and requires a smaller balance of payments outlay for imported feed grains. Within the United States, beef consumption declined from 116 pounds in 1972 to 112 pounds in 1973, and comparable declines were recorded for other meats such as pork and poultry. The decline in U.S. meat consumption was the result of a substantial increase in price, occasional empty meat counters in some parts of the country, and informal private sector rationing of limited supplies to customers by both wholesalers and retailers.

The choice of where we live is also beginning to diminish in the face of growing population pressures throughout the world. It was not too long ago in history that opportunities for migrating from one country to another were widely prevalent. Indeed, some countries encouraged immigration from more densely populated countries to build up their reservoir of skills and labor. In recent years, however, migration has become increasingly subject to various restrictions as nations become concerned with overcrowding and more selective about the immigrants they regard as economically and socially acceptable.

Even movement from rural to urban communities is becoming more difficult in many places as cities attempt to limit or discourage the rural influx once welcomed. This is true of cities as dissimilar as Denver, Oslo, Moscow, Dar es Salaam, and Djakarta. China has perhaps gone further than any other country in this respect; not only does it rigorously attempt to prevent migration into the major cities from the countryside, but periodically it deports large numbers of young people from urban to rural communities as a means of stabilizing urbanization.

More recently, the pressure on resources of continuing population growth is beginning to affect human mobility—how frequently and how far we are able to travel from home. The role of the private automobile may have reached its zenith as a form of transportation in at least some societies. The limitations on the speed at which one can travel in an automobile, often now not for reasons of safety but for reasons of energy scarcity, impinge upon our mobility. For the more affluent, there is the prospect that airlines may abolish the luxury of first-class accommodations in order to use aircraft space more efficiently and thus conserve fuel.

International travel will be curbed not only by the scarcity of energy, but quite possibly also because some countries particularly attractive to tourists will be unwilling or unable to accommodate the influx of people which unrestricted international travel would bring them. Future governments seem almost certain to impose quotas and other controls on visitors to popular tourist areas such as Mediterranean Europe, East Africa, and some of the National Parks in the United States. Over the past several years, the state of Oregon has stepped up its legal and psychological campaign to discourage visitors from lingering. For many in affluent societies, having a second home at the lake, the seashore, or in the mountains, and being able to travel there freely, involves new considerations and problems that did not exist a few years ago.

Not only the luxury of a second home, but private property rights of all kinds are being affected by the growing pressure on resources. The opportunity to own land and the freedom to use it as one sees fit may be diminishing in many nations. As the cost of building materials rises, more and more people may be forced even to abandon the notion of a private home. Single-unit dwellings may increasingly give way to multi-unit dwellings as savings in construction materials and conservation of energy become paramount. Even such routines of daily living as the disposal of waste are coming under stringent regulation. Americans are being forced to purchase automobiles with costly pollution control devices which decrease the efficiency of the engine. Many communities now have ordinances preventing the burning of leaves or trash by individuals, requiring that this function be surrendered to a municipal service agency.

These are only a few of the ways in which individual opportunities will diminish in the years ahead as population continues to grow. This should not be considered a comprehensive list; it is only a beginning, and it would be presumptuous to assume that we can even begin to anticipate all of the ways in which future population growth will impinge upon our habits, choices, and mobility.

The growing danger is that, through our present lack of urgent action on the population front, we will be ensuring a future need for ever greater regulation of human activities. As political, social, and economic systems attempt to cope with the consequences of population pressures, there will be little choice but increasingly to restrict various individual freedoms. We must now make the effort to understand more fully the alternatives facing us—our choice between a world of greater human numbers, in which societies are forced to adopt otherwise undesired measures, and a world of smaller numbers, in which societies retain more freedom to determine life styles and social designs.

Difficult Choices and Trade-offs

During the years immediately ahead, mankind will be forced to make many difficult choices and to calculate many trade-offs as a result of emerging pressures on resources of various kinds. They will take many forms and will exist at all levels—global, national, local, family, and individual. This process of calculating the trade-offs will inevitably affect attitudes and policies toward population growth at each of these levels.

At the local level, for example, it will be increasingly necessary to make choices as to how fresh-water lakes are used. The choice may be between recreation, irrigation, waste absorption, or the production of fish. Some, but not all, of these uses are compatible. If lakes are used for waste absorption, they may not be suitable for fish production or recreation purposes. The owners of homes around a lake may band together to pass an ordinance limiting the amount of fertilizer used in the vicinity, or even banning its use entirely.

A trade-off which must be calculated increasingly in the future is that between worsening air pollution and rising energy costs. Following the events of 1973, there is growing pressure to use high-sulfur fuels for the production of power and heat. In effect, the choice is between a rising incidence of respiratory illnesses such as emphysema and lung cancer on the one hand, and a more abundant supply of energy for heating, transportation, and industry on the other. The current controversy surrounding strip mining is essentially focused on the trade-off between the destruction of the natural topography and the desire for cheap energy.

Some of the trade-offs will involve conflicts between local and national governments, and between national and international interests. Should land in East Africa that is now in game preserves be maintained for that purpose, or should it gradually be shifted to food production to meet the needs of the rapidly growing populations in the nations where the reserves are located? The voters in the state of Delaware may decide (as they have) that the construction of additional oil refineries will not be in the best interests of the state. The national government in Washington may decide it is in the national interest to use the coast of Delaware to construct more oil refineries. Water resources in the northern Great Plains may be used either for agricultural purposes, as is now the case, or for coal gasification and restoration of strip-mined areas. Since there is not enough for unlimited use for both purposes, a choice must be made. Will it be made at the local level or at the national level?

The prospect of more people in the world means that there will be fewer species of wildlife. The conflict will be essentially between those who are more interested in preserving as many species of wildlife as possible and those who are interested in adequately sustaining more people.

One of the most difficult choices which must be made at the national level is the extent to which the individual should be penalized for the benefit of society. To what extent are governments morally justified in invoking such economic disincentives as limits on the number of children for which income tax deductions or rationing cards are permitted? At what point does the interest of society at large override the interest of the individual, justifying individual penalties?

Factors Influencing National Demographic Policies

Sustained rapid population growth is so recent that there has not yet been an opportunity to experience, assess, and understand what is happening to our planet. But any country maintaining a population growth rate of 3 percent for even a few generations is committing demographic suicide. By refusing to limit the size of their families, parents of today may be dooming their children and grandchildren to a subhuman level of existence.

Because of the important decisions on policies affecting population growth are made at the national level, it is useful to examine some specific factors and trends affecting national attitudes toward population growth and family planning services. National governments, many of them not yet strongly motivated to limit growth, will perceive the threat of continuing population growth in various ways. In some countries, it will be manifested in the form of intolerable levels of pollution and deepening fears of environmentally induced illnesses. In others, soaring rates of unemployment and the resulting social and political instability will goad political leaders into action. Among the other manifestations of overpopulation that may arouse governments to a sense of urgency may be food shortages, ecosystem deterioration, crowding, shortages of housing, scarcity of water, rising pressures to emigrate, growing numbers of induced abortions, growing imbalance between numbers of schools and school-age children, runaway urbanization, and diminishing per capita natural resources of all kinds.

Within the United States, the aroused awareness and resistance to continuing population growth has largely resulted from congestion, pollution, and growing pressures on natural recreation areas such as beaches and parks. In some regions of the country, the lack of water has triggered active concern. In Egypt, the event that jolted the leadership into action on the family planning front was the published finding that the population increase in the Nile River valley during the period the vast Aswan Dam was under construction would totally absorb the additional food production the dam's additional irrigation capacity would make possible. Within India, a country not overly rich in natural resources, the rising cost of importing such scarce commodities as food, energy, and fertilizer has begun to bring the already obvious population threat into even sharper focus. Not only is the volume of some imports, such as energy, necessarily rising, but in many cases the cost per unit is climbing at an astonishing rate. Soaring costs of food and energy imports could almost wholly absorb India's foreign exchange earnings, bringing the development process for which India's political leaders and economic planners have worked so long to a standstill.

Mexican political leaders became alarmed when they realized that their very impressive 7 percent rate of economic growth was simply not providing enough jobs to absorb the new entrants into the labor force. Another shock occurred when Mexico moved in the early 1970s from being a food exporter, an accomplishment made possible by the highly successful Green Revolution, to being a food importer. Learning that the exciting expansion in food output of the 1955–70 period was being washed away by the tide of a population doubling every 21 years was a sobering experience. It helped to induce an abrupt turnaround in Mexican policy in April 1972, when the government announced it was launching a nationwide family planning program.

For Japan, the wisdom of encouraging any additional population growth at all is being considered at the highest official levels. After a dramatic lowering of population growth rates during the early postwar period, the growth rate has since been gradually edging upward, until it is today double that of the United States. Pollution is becoming a serious political issue in the heavily industrialized Japanese islands, an issue quite capable of unseating a government unable to cope with it. The combination of population growth and rising affluence is putting great pressure on living space. Land prices are doubling every few years, natural recreation areas are overtaxed, and ski slopes are so crowded that they are a serious threat to physical safety. Construction of new golf courses to meet the soaring demand may be prohibited. Beaches are both polluted and overcrowded.

In both Chile and Colombia, recognition of the need for a family planning program originated within the medical community, which became alarmed at the number of hospital beds and the share of blood plasma required to repair damage resulting from botched illegal abortions. As the gap between the desire to limit family size and the availability of contraceptive services widened, the only rational response was to make family planning services available.

The grave concern over the consequences of continuing population growth in China is currently focused on food. The food-producing potential of China may have been more fully realized than that of any other major developing country. The Chinese leadership, anxious to protect its remarkable achievements in nutrition, has concluded it must apply the demographic brakes vigorously.

Within Bangladesh, the situation is more serious, for a Malthusian specter of sheer starvation hovers over the newly created nation. Few countries are as densely populated and subsist on such a marginal economic base as Bangladesh, a country of 70 million people crowded into a corner of the Indian subcontinent.

In the Soviet Union, the shortage of housing has apparently been a major factor in reducing population growth throughout much of the postwar period. Another factor limiting family size is the existence of rather abundant employment opportunities for women. For many women, professional opportunities offer an alternative means of self-fulfillment to the more traditional one of childbearing.

In Nigeria, the most populous country on the African continent, growing pressures of human and livestock populations are beginning to undermine the ecological foundations on which agriculture in the northern portion of the country rests, and the prospect of accelerating overgrazing and deforestation is now worrisome. Meanwhile, Nigeria's urban centers are mushrooming, and are increasingly characterized by extreme traffic congestion, soaring land prices, and an inability of the government to provide basic social amenities for a higher portion of city dwellers. If the demographic brakes are not applied soon, Nigeria will risk the loss of what is, particularly given its rich oil resources, a rather promising future.

Even a country as richly endowed with resources as Brazil must exercise extreme caution. It has a substantial unrealized potential, particularly in agriculture, but it must double its food production within the next eighteen years merely to keep pace with the projected internal growth in demand. As of 1973, exports of soybeans and beef were being restricted because of domestic food scarcity. It is already a heavy importer of wheat, contributing to the net cereal deficit of Latin America. Unemployment remains a critical social problem, despite extraordinary rates of industrial growth. The Brazilian experience is further evidence that a generous endowment of resources alone is not sufficient to overcome the arithmetic of continuing exponential population growth.

Population Growth: Independent or Dependent?

Given the numerous ecological and social stresses and resource scarcities emerging during the early 1970s, we must ask whether it is any longer realistic to consider population growth as a largely independent variable—whether it is realistic for demographers to project future population growth without assessing the prospect for supporting the projected populations at levels of consumption *they* find acceptable. In order to do this meaningfully, extensive inputs from several other related disciplines are required. As additional information is taken into account, the discrepancy between the projected growth in population and that which would be tolerable, or even possible, appears to be widening.

Population growth per se is not the only additional claimant on resources. The aspiration of mankind for higher consumption levels appears to be universal. We do not know what the relative roles of these two forces will be in the final quarter of this century. But we do know that the more resources required to meet the additional requirements of population growth, the less there will be for raising per capita consumption levels.

Existing demographic projections, like the economic ones, have assumed a more or less business-as-usual condition for the future periods covered by the projections. But as we analyze current ecological and social stresses and resource scarcities, even a doubling of world population without any further improvement in per capita consumption becomes a rather frightful prospect in light of the social stresses and potential political conflict that would be likely to accompany it. Similarly, a doubling of per capita consumption levels worldwide, which would still leave the world at only a fraction of North American levels, would put a great strain on the earth's resources—even assuming no further growth in population. A 50 percent increase in world population, combined with a 50 percent rise in individual affluence worldwide, would bring a *125 percent* increase in world consumption of goods and services. Even this modest growth in population, assuming it is matched by growth in per capita consumption, as was the case during the third quarter of this century, will not only further aggravate existing ecological stresses and resource scarcities, but generate many more as well.

The time has come to broaden the information and analytical base from which population projections are made. The growing scarcities of many vital resources and, more important, the reaction to these scarcities at the individual, national, and global levels, must be fully taken into account in considering future population prospects. Inputs from agronomists, ecologists, human toxicologists, meteorologists, and resource specialists must be included in future population projections, if they are to have any validity, any relationship to the real world.

As the consequences of continuing population growth become more clearly and widely understood, it seems likely that we will be forced to treat future population growth as a dependent rather than an independent variable. As it becomes more difficult and costly to achieve the inevitable balance between supply and demand by expanding the supply, it will become necessary to adjust the demand. It is in this context that efforts to stabilize population growth everywhere, and to simplify life styles among the world's more affluent, begin to loom large.

Any consideration of alternative demographic trends is in reality a consideration of alternative futures for the human race. Virtually all the important problems facing mankind will be aggravated, and their solutions made more difficult, by population growth. If a worldwide poll were conducted today asking whether people would like to see a doubling in world population, a great majority would undoubtedly respond negatively. There are now organizations in at least a few countries whose objective is zero population growth. A steadily lengthening list of governments have adopted population stability as a national goal. Some groups are urging that populations are already too large and should be reduced. In at least three countries—the United States, the United Kingdom, and the Netherlands—there are organized groups urging the adoption of national policies and of individual fertility behavior which would gradually reduce population.

People in many parts of the world would now like to see population growth slow and stabilize soon, but there is a gap between individual hopes for relief from generalized population pressure and the collective result of individual attitudes and initiatives toward childbearing. Individual couples may recognize the serious problems of overpopulation but still feel the need for several children to provide security in old age. Some may want a male heir almost regardless of how many daughters they have. Many simply do not have the education to evaluate cause and effect. The issue before the international community is how to bring national family planning programs and incentives for reduced family size, and through them individual attitudes and decisions, in line with the over-all need and desire for population stability.

12

Population Strategy for a Finite Planet

There are few if any informed people who any longer deny the need to stabilize world population. The only real issue is the timing. As noted earlier, existing UN projections indicate that world population will continue to grow until at least the end of the twenty-first century, reaching 10 billion. Many working in the population field, even while fully aware of the many adverse consequences of such a result, have tended to accept totals of this magnitude as inevitable, regardless of the consequences, since altering the trend appeared to be next to impossible.

For those who believe that the combined effect of population growth to the currently projected 10–16 billion and continuously rising affluence will put more pressure on the earth's resources and ecosystem than they can withstand, it is imperative to examine more radical alternatives. It is necessary to explore the possibilities for a different demographic future, one which holds future population growth to a sustainable level. In that spirit a world population stabilization timetable is presented in this chapter. Keeping our future numbers down to the total suggested as possible—a population stabilized at just under 6 billion in the early twenty-first century—would involve for many nations a much more abrupt shift from past trends than many have considered feasible. When weighed against the consequences of a failure to bring about such a change in habits, however, a program like that suggested below begins to appear less as an inconceivable possibility and more as an urgent necessity.

A Proposed Stabilization Timetable

It is difficult to see how any further growth in world population could enhance the quality of human existence. On the other hand, one can readily envisage ways in which further population increments will diminish our well-being. If we define optimum population as a level beyond which further increases would no longer improve the quality of human life, then world population has already passed the optimum level. As our concern over the quality of life escalates, this concept becomes more useful than the more traditional calculations of the planet's carrying capacity, a concept which ignores the quality of human existence.

An abrupt slowdown in population growth can be both socially and economically disruptive, just as the explosive growth in the group under 15 years of age is today overwhelming educational and health services and the current and projected capacity of the poorer countries to create jobs. Any strategy to stabilize world population growth represents a compromise between the benefits of stabilizing population immediately, as dictated by ecological, resource, or quality-of-life considerations, and the recognition that the required changes in human behavior will not occur overnight, even under optimal circumstances.

Because of the sharp contrast in current fertility levels between the developed and less developed countries, it is useful to separate these two groups of countries for strategy purposes. In the more developed countries, where populations are growing slowly, it should be possible to achieve stability much sooner than in less developed countries, where population growth rates generally remain rather high and the proportion of the population at childbearing age is also high. Nearly a score of developed countries are already below or are approaching replacement level fertility.

Three European countries—West Germany, East Germany, and Luxembourg—have achieved population stability within the past few years (see Table 17). Births and deaths in these three countries, with a combined population of 79 million, are essentially in balance. Another group of more developed countries, containing 310 million people, have birth rates that are low and declining. This group of countries—including Austria, Belgium, the United Kingdom, Sweden, Finland, Hungary, and the United States—could attain population stability by 1980, if the recent decline in birth rates continues. Given the low birth rates now existing in most industrial countries, a relatively modest further reduction in the crude birth rate would result in population stability. It is not unreasonable, then, to suggest that *all the more developed countries should strive for population stability not later than 1985.*

The basic pattern suggested for the more developed nations is portrayed by the trend in West German birth and death rates since 1960 (see Figure 7). The number of births per thousand of population fell from 18.5 in the early 1960s to 10.4 in 1973. Meanwhile the death rate remained fairly stable, generally staying between 11 and 12. West Germany's population stopped growing in 1971, East Germany's even earlier, in the late 1960s.

In the United States, the birth rate has declined even more rapidly than in West Germany, falling from 23.7 in 1960 to 15.0 in 1973 (see Figure 8). Since the 1973 death rate was 9.4, the U.S. population was still growing at about one-half percent annually. If the particularly steep downward trend in the U.S. birth rate since 1970 is maintained, the lines will cross and zero population growth will be attained before the end of this decade. The birth rate in Canada, below 16 in 1972, is also declining very rapidly.

Table 17. Countries Achieving or Approaching Population Stability, 1973

	POPULATION	CRUDE BIRTH RATE	CRUDE DEATH RATE	ANNUAL RATE OF NATURAL INCREASE
	(million)			(percent)
East Germany	17	11.7	13.9	−0.22
West Germany	62	10.6	11.9	−0.13
Luxembourg	.3	11.4	12.4	−0.10
Austria	7	13.4	12.6	+0.08
Belgium	10	13.6	12.5	+0.11
United Kingdom	56	14.7	11.9	+0.28
Finland	5	12.4	9.6	+0.28
Sweden	8	13.4	10.3	+0.31
Hungary	10	14.7	11.5	+0.32
United States	208	15.0	9.4	+0.56
Switzerland	6	14.8	9.4	+0.54

SOURCE: Preliminary estimates based on United Nations data.

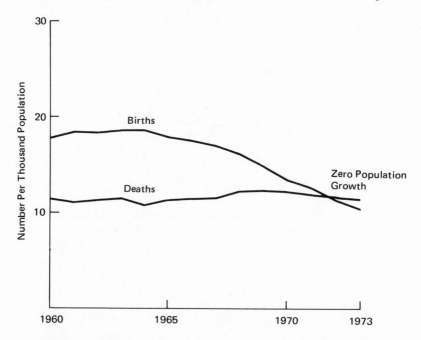

Figure 7
Birth and Death Rates in West Germany, 1960–1973

Source: United Nations

The United Kingdom is even closer to stability than the United States. Its birth rate has also shown a downward trend, declining from 18.8 in 1964 to 14.7 in 1973. With an older population than the United States, its death rate is higher—11.9—resulting in an annual growth rate of only .28 percent. Vital statistics in the Soviet Union in the mid-1970s, with a birth rate of 18 and a death rate of 9, resemble those of the United States in 1967. Japan's population is growing at just over 1 percent per year, but the declining number of young people entering the reproductive years, as a result of the sharp drop in fertility from 1948 to 1955, means population stabilization is a readily achievable goal.

Within the developing world, at least ten countries have succeeded in reducing their birth rates in a steady, sustained fashion by well over one birth per thousand per year for an extended period. In some countries, it has been much closer to two. These countries, listed in

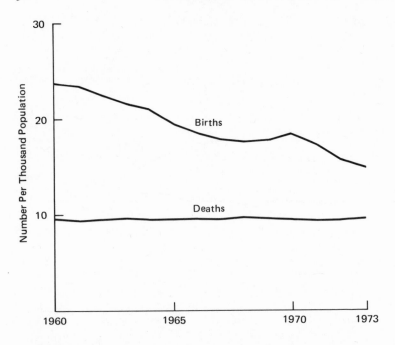

Figure 8
Birth and Death Rates in the United States, 1960–1973

Source: United Nations

Table 18, represent a broad cross section of the developing world in terms of geography, political system, and prevailing religion. Some are in Asia, some in Africa, and some in Latin America; some are Temperate Zone, others tropical. National religions include Protestant, Catholic, Buddhist, and Muslim. Populations range from less than a million in Barbados to 35 million each in Korea and Egypt.

Social needs appear to be more fully satisfied in these countries than in most developing countries. With the exception of Tunisia and Egypt, literacy levels tend to be near the upper end of the spectrum, but even though the Tunisian and Egyptian rates are relatively low on a worldwide scale, they are among the highest in Africa. Infant mortality is also substantially lower in this group of countries than in most developing countries. Each of these nations has a reasonably well-organized, strongly supported family planning program, though in many cases birth rates started falling even before major family planning efforts got under way.

Once the genuine urgency of slowing population growth is recognized, and given the record already established by several less developed countries, it should be possible for all less developed countries making the appropriate effort *to reduce birth rates to 25 per thousand by 1985.* If the less developed countries could accomplish this in the next eleven years, a much smaller age group would enter the prime reproductive ages between 2005 and 2015; at that stage, it should be possible to take the final step, bringing the birth rate into balance with the death rate. Up to 2005, birth rates in most less developed nations would remain at about where the U.S., West German, and Soviet birth rates were in the early 1960s (20–25 per thousand). From then until 2015, they would essentially be repeating what we have suggested above for the developed countries between 1975 and 1985—bringing moderate growth down to zero.

The notion of reducing crude birth rates in the less developed countries to 25 per thousand by 1985 is extraordinarily ambitious. It will require much more rapid changes in fertility than most observers have considered possible. But if we examine the performance of those of the less developed countries which have been most successful in reducing population growth rates, then it begins to appear a much more feasible goal.

Table 18. Crude Birth Rate Decline
in Selected Developing Countries

COUNTRY	TIME SPAN	AVERAGE ANNUAL DECLINE IN CRUDE BIRTH RATE	CRUDE BIRTH RATE, 1972
		(births per thousand per year)	
Barbados	1960–69	1.5	22
Taiwan	1955–71	1.2	24
Tunisia	1966–71	1.8	35
Mauritius	1961–71	1.5	25
Hong Kong	1960–72	1.4	19
Singapore	1955–72	1.2	23
Costa Rica	1963–72	1.5	32
South Korea	1960–70	1.2	29
Egypt	1966–70	1.7	37
Chile	1963–70	1.2	25

SOURCE: United Nations and U.S. Agency for International Development.

It is useful to remind ourselves that six developing countries had already reduced their crude birth rates to 25 per thousand or less by 1973. These six countries, all smaller ones, are Mauritius, Singapore, Hong Kong, Taiwan, Barbados, and Trinidad and Tobago, a group which has a total population of 24 million. Another group of countries had crude birth rates of 30 or less by 1973: Sri Lanka, quite possibly China, South Korea, Cuba, and Chile, with a combined population of 862 million. Thus, eleven countries with a combined population of 886 million may have achieved birth rates of 30 or below by 1973. Argentina and Uruguay, two other Southern Hemisphere countries with relatively high average incomes, both have achieved crude birth rates below 25.

The timetable proposed for fertility reductions in less developed nations between now and 1985 is quite consistent with the goals set by governments in many countries with officially stated objectives. National family planning goals are variously formulated—in terms of reductions in crude birth rates, in terms of the over-all population growth rate, or in terms of reaching a certain proportion of the population with family planning services. During the early 1970s, Egypt adopted a goal of reducing its crude birth rate by one point per year over the next ten years, a goal consistent with the 1985 target. India's stated goal has been to reduce its birth rate from 39 in 1968 to 25 in 1981, four years ahead of our 1985 target. Though it has fallen behind its own timetable, fertility is declining and it could still meet our more modest timetable.

Indonesia's recently launched family planning program has a target of 6 million acceptors of family planning services during its 1971–75 five year plan. Chile seeks an increase in couples using contraception from 18 percent in 1971 to 30 percent by 1976. Bangladesh's first five year plan aims to prevent 1.5 million births in five years, and to achieve zero population growth within thirty years.

An examination of trends in Taiwan and Chile (Figures 9 and 10) helps illustrate the pattern called for in the less developed nations over the next eleven years. Taiwan's birth rate, now at 24, has fallen rather consistently since the early 1950s, when it ranged from 45 to 50 births per thousand. Because of a youthful population and widespread health care, Taiwan's death rate is just 5, so its population is still growing at 1.9 percent annually. Since the birth rate was very high throughout the 1950s, when today's parents were born, it will be very difficult for Taiwan to push its birth rate below 20 in the next decade. But as the age groups born since the mid-1960s, when birth rates have been much lower, enter childbearing age, further reductions in Taiwan's birth rate will be much easier to accomplish. As the end of the century draws near and the larger age groups approach old age, the death rate will gradually rise, further easing the attainment of population stability.

To meet the timetable presented, other less developed nations will have to reduce birth rates by 1985 to a level comparable to that of Taiwan in 1972. For many larger nations, including India, Thailand, Burma, Egypt, and Turkey, with birth rates of between 35 and 40— the same as Taiwan's in the early 1960s—this will mean dupli-

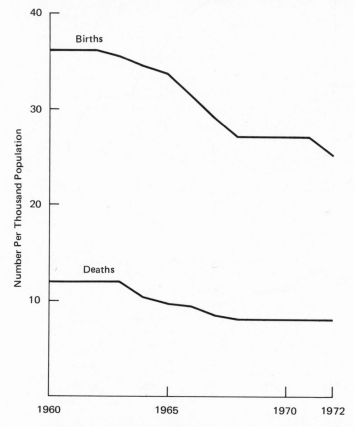

Figure 9
Birth and Death Rates in Chile, 1960–1972

Source: United Nations and U.S. Agency for International Development

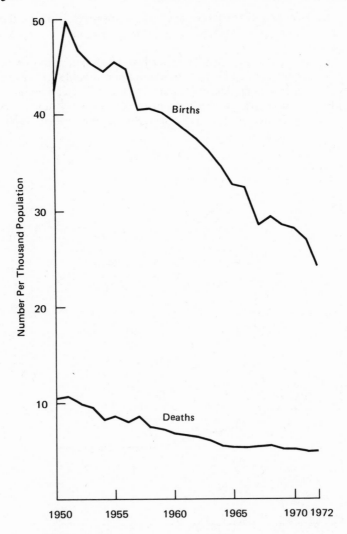

Figure 10
Birth and Death Rates in Taiwan, 1950–1972

Source: United Nations and U.S. Agency for International Development

cating during the coming decade the birth rate decline experienced by
Taiwan over the last decade. In other nations, such as Indonesia,

Bangladesh, Pakistan, the Philippines, and many African nations, the decline will have to be even more rapid.

Chile's birth rate dropped from 36 in the early 1960s to 25 in 1972. Brazil, with a birth rate of 37, will have to duplicate this decline by 1985. Mexico and Colombia, both with birth rates of 43, will have to reduce their birth rates at a faster pace.

Some knowledgeable observers may well declare the target proposed for the less developed nations to be "unattainable." However, consideration of the population size with which many nations will be burdened *even if they meet these stringent goals* makes the prospect of not meeting them equally impossible to imagine. We then have little choice but to adjust our family planning goals and the scale of our efforts to meet them.

Under our proposed timetable, China, already becoming dependent on grain imports to preserve adequate nutrition among its 800 million people, would reach a total of 1.33 billion just four decades from now. India, already struggling to feed and maintain political and economic order among a population of under 600 million, would have to cope with nearly a billion in 2015. Bangladesh, badly overcrowded and existing on a threadbare margin of survival in 1974 with an estimated population of 77 million, would have to find means of supporting an additional 50 million people.

Mexico, already dependent on the illegal emigration of an estimated quarter of a million workers annually to the United States to help alleviate its unemployment crisis, would grow from 55 to 103 million people. Nigeria would face an increase in numbers from 55 million to nearly 100 million as well. Egypt, now with a population of about 35 million, would still have to squeeze an additional 26 million people into the slender Nile valley if it meets our timetable.

Under the proposed timetable (Table 19), the substantial declines in birth rates between 1975 and 1985 in both the developed and less developed countries, as the former group moved to population stability and the latter lowered their crude birth rate to 25, would reduce the annual world population growth rate from 1.9 percent in 1970 to 1.1 percent in 1985. This decade would be one

Table 19. A Proposed Population
Stabilization Timetable

	1970	1975	1985	2000	2005	2015
World population (billions)	3.6	3.9	4.5	5.3	5.5	5.8
Annual growth rate (percent)	1.9	1.7	1.1	1.0	.9	0
Annual increase (millions)	69	65	50	52	49	0

of steadily declining fertility throughout the world.

Despite continuing stringent efforts, there would be little further decline from 1985 to the end of the century, as populations in the more developed countries would already have stabilized while the large age groups resulting from the large number of births during the 1960–75 period in the less developed countries would be in the prime reproductive years. The second phase of the push toward stabilization would come during the decade from 2005 to 2015, when the sharply reduced group born after 1985 would be entering the prime reproductive years. This would yield a stabilized world population of just under 6 billion by 2015. Even with these extraordinary efforts, the 1970 world population would have increased by nearly two-thirds.

The timetable assumes that birth rates in China will follow the same pattern as those in other developing nations—falling to 25 in 1985, with the population not stabilizing until 2015. Given the urgency with which the Chinese leadership is currently addressing the population threat, however, there is a good possibility that China will progress well ahead of our timetable, that its growth will taper off much more sharply than we have assumed. Exceeding the target reduction in fertility in China will help offset any possible failures to meet the timetable in other nations. Also, the timetable makes no allowance for possible negative growth rates in some more developed nations. In 1973, the population of East and West Germany combined actually declined by 115,000, because the birth rate dropped below the death rate. Over the next forty years, it is highly likely that such situations will emerge in other societies as well.

Most demographers have viewed replacement level fertility, an average family slightly above two children, as the lower limit on national fertility reductions, primarily because there is little historical precedent for a sustained fertility level much below that. The UN projections cited previously assume the attainment and maintenance of replacement levels in all nations by the mid-twenty-first century. But meeting the timetable proposed here will require the reduction of fertility levels to below replacement in many societies for at least a period of years. In some countries, it will mean that for short periods the average family size may be closer to one child than to two. This is obviously not an easily attainable target. It implies changes in human fertility behavior more comprehensive than any in history. It can only be accomplished through extraordinary global efforts to change attitudes, to ensure the universal availability of family planning services, and to reorient national and international economic policies toward meeting the basic social needs of all people.

Filling the Family Planning Gap

A distressingly large share of the world's fertile population does not have ready access to family planning services. In some instances, this is because the services are not locally available, in other instances because they are too costly for many who want and need them. Within the more developed countries, the problem is not lack of sufficient resources to provide family planning services to all who require them, regardless of income level, but rather that policies and internal priorities have been focused elsewhere. For example, only since 1970, with passage of the Family Planning Services and Population Research Act, has the United States moved systematically to ensure the availability of family planning services to all Americans regardless of geographic location or economic status.

Among the less developed countries, the ready availability of family planning services that reach the majority are still the exception rather than the rule. The United Nations Fund for Population Activities (UNFPA) estimates that the cost of providing family planning services ranges between 50 cents and one dollar per year per capita for an entire population. The actual cost per capita to those who need advice and contraceptives is several times higher, since the group at risk is only a small fraction of the total population.

The only populous less developed country which appears largely to have overcome the logistical and economic obstacles to providing family planning services is the People's Republic of China. If we exclude China from our considerations, the remaining less developed countries contain roughly 2 billion people. Using the UNFPA estimate for the cost of providing family planning services of one dollar per person, this would then require $2 billion to provide universal family planning services. If one-half of this were to come from internal resources and one-half from external resources, roughly a billion dollars would be required annually from the international community. These funds would be used for training of personnel, for educational materials, for clinics, for transportation equipment (including jeeps and bicycles), and for provision of contraceptives.

Given the enormous unsatisfied demand for family planning services in the world, there is probably no expenditure of funds which can approach the effectiveness of family planning services in breaking the self-reinforcing cycle of poverty and high fertility. Based on surveys covering desired and actual family size in the developing world, the Population Council reports that *if* the responses were genuine, and *if* family planning programs could satisfy this demand, then birth rates in the developing world would fall by some nine to twelve points. In global economic terms, the expenditure is quite small; in terms of its impact on human well-being, it can be of profound importance. The present flow of funds into the less developed countries from both public and private sources for family planning purposes approximates $250 million, scarcely a quarter of what is needed.

It would be naïve to claim that the mere availability of $2 billion for global family planning programs would result in the immediate filling of the world family planning gap. Obviously, major organizational and political problems would still plague the effort to make family planning services universally available. The point to be underscored, however, is that, given the appropriate international political will, the *financial* resources required by a global family planning effort would be almost insignificant in global economic terms. They would be trivial when compared with existing military expenditures of national governments, yet the threat to our future well-being of uncontrolled human fertility may be greater than that of international aggression.

Commercial Distribution of Contraceptives

Because family planning initiatives and programs at the national level usually originate with governments in the developing nations, there is a tendency to overlook the potential role of the commercial sector in the distribution of contraceptives. For several reasons, the distribution potential of the commercial sector ought to be harnessed in efforts to make family planning services available to everyone. One reason is that commercial channels already supply an estimated 40 percent of all contraceptives used in the less developed world, and an even larger proportion in the developed countries. Another is that personnel costs, which often eat up 90 percent of the funds of family planning programs, and organizational difficulties are greatly reduced by capitalizing on existing services and channels of distribution. The local availability of reasonably priced contraceptives through familiar commercial outlets helps ensure that motivation does not get very far ahead of services, as the near epidemic level of induced abortions in many countries would indicate is now the case.

Whenever possible, commercial distribution systems should augment government programs. Even if there is a need to subsidize distribution of contraceptives or to distribute them free, commercial

Table 20. Non-Commercial and Commercial Distribution of Contraceptives in Six Developing Countries in 1971

	SHARE OF TARGET POPULATION USING CONTRACEPTIVES	SHARE OBTAINED FROM NON-COMMERCIAL SOURCES	COMMERCIAL SOURCES
South Korea	31.1	25.5	5.6
Thailand	16.0	6.5	9.5
Iran	15.0	8.5	6.5
Venezuela	9.6	1.5	8.1
Philippines	8.7	6.1	2.6
Turkey	7.3	2.8	4.5

SOURCE: Westinghouse Population Center, *The Victor-Bostrom Fund Report,* no. 16, Winter 1972–73.

outlets may be able to do at least a certain amount of this at much less cost than government-operated programs. The existence of commercial services satisfies the needs of a sizable segment of the population, sometimes a major segment, freeing official resources and programs to concentrate on those not otherwise reached. Even economically advanced countries such as the United States need official programs to reach those whose need for advice and contraceptives is not satisfied by commercial services.

In many countries, no additional investment whatever is required in order to harness the potential of the indigenous commercial system for the countrywide distribution of low-cost contraceptives. In some instances, it is necessary or at least helpful to remove any import restrictions and duties on contraceptives. In other countries, it is essential that present requirements for medical prescriptions be removed in order for the pill to be successfully marketed commercially. It is difficult to justify the prescription requirement for recognized brands of oral contraceptives which have been tested and released for unrestricted commercial use in the more developed countries. Apart from the cost, the shortage of physicians has the effect of prohibiting the use of this modern, highly effective contraceptive by tens of millions of low-income women.

Some government programs work with commercial networks to distribute contraceptives at a subsidized rate. The government or some other organization may, for example, provide the contraceptives free to the commercial distributor, requiring only that he sell as widely as possible at an agreed-upon price which would cover his costs and permit an adequate profit.

Creating Social Conditions for Fertility Decline

Filling the gap between the demand for family planning services and their availability as rapidly as possible is essential, but it is not enough. Although this will contribute to a significant decline in fertility in virtually every society, it is not likely to reduce markedly the fertility of that preponderant share of humanity suffering from severe social deprivation. Unless a way can be found to satisfy the basic social needs of this group, the chances of attaining the desperately needed decline in fertility are almost nonexistent.

Throughout the quarter century since foreign assistance began, efforts to assist the less developed countries have been conceived in terms of narrowing the economic gap between rich countries and poor. Now, at a time when the relationship between well-being and the consumption of material goods is being reexamined in all societies, the problem needs to be redefined. The gap to be narrowed between the more developed and less developed countries as rapidly as possible is in the area of basic social needs. The key indicators become social rather than strictly economic—the level of literacy, infant mortality, life expectancy, and the opportunity for productive employment. In Chapter 9, the outlines of a broad national strategy to improve the economic and social welfare of the poor within less developed nations were presented. In this section, we shall discuss more specifically potential internationally supported strategies to focus directly on key social needs.

Literacy is one of the easiest social needs to satisfy if governments are fully committed to this goal. In part, this is because most resources required to achieve universal literacy are available within the developing countries themselves, and also because imparting literacy is a one-time effort (unlike health services, which must be provided on a continuous basis). In those countries in which successful literacy efforts have been launched, teachers, civil servants, in some cases the army, and volunteers from among recent university graduates have been among those mobilized for the campaign. A number of success stories can be cited of countries that have progressed steadily and rapidly from being largely illiterate to becoming largely literate, including China since 1949 and Cuba in the early 1960s. More recently, Brazil has launched a vigorous program.

Although the cost of achieving universal literacy cannot be precisely estimated, there is reason to believe that it may be much less than might be imagined. In the 1960s, UNESCO estimated the cost of enabling a person to become literate in a developing country at about $8, slightly less for an adult, slightly more for a school-age youngster. Given the nearly billion illiterates in the less developed countries, the elimination of illiteracy would require an outlay of $8 billion. If a program were spread over five years, the cost would come to $1.6 billion a year. And if the cost were allocated among the principal industrial countries, no one country would have to contribute more than a few hundred million dollars a year. The benefits to those becoming literate and to mankind as a whole are enormous, especially if one takes into account the effect of literacy on receptivity to family planning. As with family planning services, the financial costs of an effort to eliminate illiteracy are by no means prohibitive. What is lacking is the appropriate degree of national and international will and organization.

Perhaps the most pressing social need of all is for an adequate, assured food supply. Poorly nourished societies are, without exception, the ones with the highest rates of infant mortality, the shortest life expectancy, and the highest birth rates. Given the close relationship between the incidence of malnutrition and high birth rates, any effort which effectively reduces malnutrition will directly contribute toward the stabilization of population growth. The mounting evidence that assured food supplies bring birth rates down, by offering greater assurance that existing children will survive, lends new urgency to efforts to expand food output in the less developed countries where supplies are most tenuous.

Anything less than a crash effort will not be satisfactory. The pressing need is to accelerate rural development in the developing countries, for this is where half of mankind lives. In this light, the recent shift in emphasis by the U.S. Agency for International Development and the World Bank to increase aid for rural development is encouraging. New programs for extending multiple cropping and other innovations of the Green Revolution need to be exploited as rapidly as possible.

Intensified efforts to expand agricultural production can have a multiple payoff if the strategy is properly designed. Small farms in the developing nations, when properly supported with credit, marketing, technical advisory services and inputs, generally are not only more efficient producers of food but also provide more jobs per acre than large estates cultivated with heavy equipment. Worldwide, malnutrition is closely associated with poverty. The greater provision of meaningful employment opportunities associated with broad-based rural development will help put purchasing power in the hands of those who most need it, as well as increase total food supplies.

Great potential is also developing for international cooperation in accelerating the production of chemical fertilizers, particularly nitrogen fertilizer. Several Middle Eastern countries with large quantities of capital are still flaring natural gas, the basic feed stock in the manufacture of nitrogen fertilizer. If the technologies of North American companies, which have developed efficient new processes for synthesizing nitrogen fertilizer, could be combined with the capital and natural gas now available in the Middle East, great quantities of low-cost fertilizer could be produced for use in the less developed countries.

The world food economy has become highly unstable during the early 1970s as world reserves of food have been depleted. The circumstances call for creation of a new international food reserve system. Just as the U.S. dollar can no longer serve as the foundation of the international monetary system, so U.S. agriculture no longer has sufficient capacity to ensure reasonable stability in the world food economy.

Perhaps the most practical way to create an effective food reserve is to construct a network of national reserves, with the level of reserves to be held in each country determined through international consultation. The sum of these national reserves would then constitute a buffer against drought, crop disease, flooding, or other disaster occurring anywhere in the world. Such a system of global food reserves would provide a measure of price stability and security in the world food economy that would be in the self-interest of all nations. The world community's basic humanitarian interest in ensuring that famine does not occur in the densely populated low-income countries following a poor crop year must not be left to the good will of the affluent nations. As long as the current system of autonomous nationally oriented food planning is allowed to continue without modification, the affluent nations may not always be able to deal with future emergencies as they have in the past. The proposal of FAO Director-General A. H. Boerma for the international coordination of national food reserve policies, which received preliminary international approval at the FAO Conference in late 1973, needs to be finally approved and put into action as soon as possible.

Under any world reserve system, special provisions will be necessary to assist developing countries to build up their own reserves. Bilateral food aid programs, particularly that of the United States, which has been by far the largest, could play a major role in meeting this need. International agencies such as the World Bank, International Monetary Fund, UNDP, and FAO should also help poor countries establish and maintain the local reserve stocks necessary for protection against crop shortfalls and failures. Without this greater degree of food security, it will be difficult to create the over-all sense of social security associated with adequate voluntary declines in fertility.

As of the mid-1970s, following a quarter century of dramatic medical advances, an estimated one-third to one-half of mankind still lives without access to health services of any kind. At least rudimentary health services, of the kind now being made available by barefoot doctors in China, must now be considered one of mankind's basic social rights. Being born human should be the only requirement for eligibility. At a minimum, health services provided should include protection against infectious diseases through vaccinations, provision of safe water supplies throughout each country, and the practice of basic public health measures in the area of preventive medicine.

A proposal for combining health and family planning services in a maternal and child health program designed specifically for developing countries has been offered by Howard C. Taylor and Bernard Berelson in a study prepared for the Population Council in New York. This program has the dual objective of improving the health of mothers and infants and providing modern contraception without charge where necessary. Education in infant care and family planning would begin during pregnancy and continue after birth.

For the average developing country, the cost per capita of the Taylor-Berelson program was estimated in the late 1960s at about 60 cents per year. Calculated in terms of care per pregnant woman, this would come to $14 per pregnancy. These costs include both the annual budgetary costs and the cost of physical facilities spread over a ten-year period. If China is excluded, for the simple reason that it is already well on its way to achieving this goal, a worldwide program for all developing countries would cost roughly $2 billion per year. Although most anticipated supportive costs are rising, an important exception is the contraceptives themselves, which tend to decline in price as patents expire and as economies of scale reduce production costs per unit.

The institutional nucleus and a reservoir of experience for launching an effort of this nature already exists in the form of the International Postpartum Program, sponsored by the Population Council. In the Postpartum Program, family planning is associated with delivery and postpartum care in large maternity hospitals in urban centers around the world. The program began in 1966 in 25 hospitals in 19 cities and 14 countries and has grown to include just over a hundred hospitals, including country networks in Colombia, Venezuela, and India. Nearly a quarter of a million new participants in family planning were enrolled during the program's first two years of operation.

If the provision for maternal, child health, and family planning services were to become nationwide in the developing countries, it would be necessary to go far beyond this network of urban hospitals, creating an auxiliary network of clinics and subclinics in many smaller communities where they do not now exist, in order to ensure access for rural as well as urban populations. It would be necessary to utilize paramedical personnel with varying levels of training, including mid-wives. The maternal and child health care centers could be operated either independently or as part of a health center providing a broader range of services. At least one auxiliary nurse-midwife would be needed in each subclinic.

Assuming a ratio of 30 midwives for each 100,000 people, this would require 300 midwives for each million of total population, or 600,000 auxiliary nurse-midwives for the total population of 2 billion in the developing countries. Even though the nucleus of such a corps already exists in some countries, recruiting and training a group of field workers on this scale is no small matter. It represents a body of skilled manpower comparable in size to the army of India.

The Future Role of Women

There are two factors which promise a profound change in the role of women in society during the decades immediately ahead. One is the desire by a steadily growing share of the world's women to have social and political rights and economic opportunities equal to those of men. The second is the pressure of population on the earth's resources, a pressure that is rapidly approaching a point at which it may not be feasible for virtually all women to bear children.

In order to reduce fertility to the levels proposed earlier, average fertility levels in some societies, for at least a limited period of time, will have to fall well below replacement. If a substantial share of the women in any given society seek alternative methods of self-fulfill-ment to childbearing, this fertility goal could be much more easily attained.

There is evidence that this is beginning to happen within the United States. In a poll taken in 1973 among young women in the senior class at Stanford University, in California, less than one in 25 said they expected to become full-time housewives within five years of gradua-tion. Because of its high academic standards and high tuition, the students of Stanford should not be considered representative of all young people in the United States. Nonetheless, the response does reflect a pronounced change in attitude among young women in the United States. Young women graduating from many American colleges today simply do not conceive of their role in society in the same way that their mothers did. They no longer automatically accept the traditional role assigned to them by society.

In such countries as West Germany, East Germany, and the Soviet Union (particularly its European portion), abundant employment opportunities for women are beginning to compete with the traditional roles of childbearing and child rearing. The result is a drop in the level of fertility well below replacement. The average woman of reproductive age is bearing fewer than the two children required to replace her and her husband. The one-child family is becoming commonplace.

The movement toward a more equitable role in society for women is not limited to the economically advanced countries. There are stirrings of the women's liberation movement in virtually every country in the world, including some of the most traditional societies, where the role of women has been very carefully circumscribed. Women's organizations devoted to securing equal rights for women are being formed even in such restrictive societies as Afghanistan and Morocco. The First National Women's Congress in Brazil, representing the women's liberation movement there, was convened late in 1972. This conference, held publicly in a traditional, male-dominated society, attracted a great deal of attention. The week-long conference discussed and debated many issues, but on two there was strong agreement—the need for planned parenthood and for day-care centers.

Changes in the role of women in society call for associated changes in the role of men. One of the difficulties married women still face in most industrial societies is that equal opportunities in the job market do not guarantee equal sharing of work on the home front.

In most societies where women have made great progress in broadening the economic and social opportunities, political equality has lagged. Though women have achieved the right to vote in most industrial societies, the share of offices which they hold is little more than a token in most countries.

Given the need to reduce fertility and birth rates, it is now imperative for every society to create employment opportunities for women sufficiently attractive to induce many of them to opt for these rather than for childbearing. Laws, customs, and regulations restricting women's rights to employment, to own property, to vote, to hold political office, and to pursue certain traditionally "male" professions must be stricken from the books. From production brigades in China to university campuses in the United States, women are beginning to perceive a future role in society quite different from that of the past. We appear to be on the verge of a major restructuring of society, a restructuring that seems inevitable, given both the desire of women for a more equitable role and the pressing need to reduce fertility throughout the world. In the future, more and more women can be expected to strive for a role in society virtually indistinguishable from that of men. They should be encouraged and assisted in every way, for it is in both their interest and that of society that they do so.

Other Policies Affecting Family Size

The universal availability of family planning services, the meeting of basic social needs, and the encouragement of new roles for women in society are the most important broad areas for action if birth rates are to be reduced rapidly. In addition, however, careful attention must be given to the national structure of economic and social incentives that affect attitudes on family size. In many nations, a large variety of policies serve to provide indirect incentives for larger families, often even as the nation adopts the goal of reducing the rate of population growth.

Income-tax deductions for an unlimited number of children, such as are currently offered in the United States, child care allowances, such as are offered in France; and unlimited subsidized maternity leaves and benefits may all create a milieu in which couples at the very least feel no incentive to hold down family size, or perhaps even feel encouraged to have more children. Strictly limiting the provision of such benefits to, say, the first two children can on the other hand help make couples think twice before having more children than needed for replacement. Measures with a similar effect would include limitations on government-subsidized housing or scholarships after the second child.

Governments can go one step further and provide positive inducements for smaller families. Special tax bonuses or cash payments can be given to those remaining single rather than penalizing them with extra taxes as is now often the case. Special pension payments can be offered as an alternative source of old-age security to those who opt to remain childless, or to limit the number of children to one or two. Measures such as these can be extended to cover all citizens, whereas tax policies have an impact only on those who are integrated into the modern economy.

The natural desire of parents to ensure the survival of children to help care for them in old age points up the crucial role that social security measures can play in reducing desired family size. Nationwide, compulsory social security programs in most economically advanced nations have greatly reduced parental economic dependence on their children, and thus indirectly have helped create the climate in which birth rates have fallen. Many poorer nations may lack the administrative and fiscal capacity to undertake an identical approach. However, imaginative new approaches are appearing which illustrate the potential for improved social security in even the poorest of nations.

One program which combines social security with positive incentives to limit births is the "savings account for family planning" designed by Ronald Ridker and being carried out in the tea estates of India. The tea estates are required by law to provide substantial maternity and child care benefits. These include not only hospitalization and medical care for the mother and infant but also long-term food, clothing, schooling, and medical care for the child. Good vital records, hospitals, family clinics, and doctors are available on all of the estates.

Under the savings scheme, the tea estate management offers each woman of childbearing age a savings account into which the firm will pay a specified amount for each month that the woman is not pregnant. The woman employee makes no payments into the account, but she is not eligible to withdraw the savings until her childbearing years are over. If she does become pregnant, the company ceases payments for a specified period and also reclaims part of its past payments into her account. These retroactive deductions are graduated according to the number of the woman's additional births, and are reclaimed by the company to help defray its expenses for these births.

What the tea estates are in effect doing is offering their women employees a choice. They can continue to receive the maternity and health benefits to which they are entitled for an unlimited number of children. Or, by deciding to limit family size, they can opt to receive the resultant savings in the form of savings for their retirement and old age. Encouragingly, the option of limiting children in exchange for old-age financial security is proving highly popular.

In China, the availability of support from one's production team may be providing a crucial measure of old-age security for both urban and rural workers. In many less developed nations a similar kind of security could be provided through farmers' cooperatives or factory savings/retirement schemes.

Policies that help raise the average age of marriage also help reduce fertility rates. Possible approaches include educational programs on both the individual and social advantages of later marriage, raising the minimum legal marriage age, levying a heavy marriage license tax for those below a certain age, and instituting such activities as compulsory service in a national service corps for young people prior to marriage.

Many measures that would raise awareness about population problems and help reduce fertility involve very little expenditure on the part of governments. Population and family planning can be introduced as a normal part of school curricula within the existing educational framework. Existing training programs for health workers and paramedics or midwives can be broadened to include elementary family planning concepts without great cost. National communications media can be encouraged to provide information on the adverse effects of population growth, the availability and proper use of contraceptives, and the positive personal incentives for smaller families.

Once family planning services are within reach of all citizens and strong efforts are under way to meet basic needs, it is important for every government to carefully examine the total structure of incentives regarding family size which its laws and institutions present to the individual. The object must be to design a broad framework of positive inducements to limit family size, and negative incentives to discourage large families. Such an incentive structure can perform an extremely effective educational function, alerting all citizens to the government's concern with population growth. It also provides a compromise between the societal need to limit population growth and the desire to preserve as much individual freedom of action as possible in a matter so personal as the size of one's family. The structure of economic incentives makes clear the societal need, and rewards those who act in accordance with it. Those who, for one reason or another, still have large families bear a share of the costs of their decision.

The poorest elements within some societies may be the least quick to reduce family size, raising the possibility that a meaningful incentive structure may help serve to perpetuate the poverty—and hence the tendency toward higher fertility—of some disadvantaged groups. This dilemma is a real one, but the net benefits, both to these groups and to the nation, outweigh this possible short-run negative consequence of incentives that strongly encourage small families. This problem particularly underlines the need for strenuous efforts to meet the social needs and improve the economic opportunities of the poor within each society. Slowing population growth will make meeting the needs of the poor easier, providing an important justification for a discriminatory incentive structure.

13

Only One Option

The proposed timetable for stabilizing world population under 6 billion represents a radical departure from present thinking in the demographic community. It is certain to elicit both criticism and skepticism. On that there is little doubt. But the central question is not whether the timetable is radical, but what the alternatives are.

Where population is concerned, we have only one option. Robert McNamara has articulated it well: "The population problem will be solved one way or another. Our only option is whether it is to be solved rationally and humanely, or irrationally and inhumanely." Continuing on the current demographic path, toward the world population of 12 billion that UN demographers now term "most likely," will not yield a humane solution to the problem. The danger signals all about us indicate that we continue on our present path only at extreme risk.

Stabilizing world population under 6 billion will not be easy, but neither is it impossible. Difficult though this may seem, it appears to be much more manageable than adequately feeding, educating, and employing the phenomenal increases in population suggested by even the lowest United Nations projections of future population.

The organizing theme of this book, written for World Population Year, is the population threat. Coping with this threat poses a basic challenge to the human community. But the population threat can be realistically and usefully approached only in a broad context, as one of several areas where basic changes in direction are called for. Thus as we prepare for the final quarter of this century we find mankind at a critical crossroads.

At the Crossroads Again

In some ways the mid-1970s resemble the early 1930s. Soaring prices of energy and food during the mid-1970s are contributing to accelerating worldwide inflation and to convulsive economic and political changes. These in turn are putting great stress on the international economic system and on political relationships among countries. During periods of stress there is a strong temptation for governments to turn inward, seeking national solutions to problems which have only international solutions. Governments succumbed to this temptation in the 1930s, erecting high tariff walls and engaging in competitive devaluations of their currencies, and thus greatly intensified the Great Depression. This turning inward and seeking national solutions to global problems did not work in the 1930s, and there is far less prospect that it would work today.

Although there is a similarity between the mid-1970s and the early 1930s, the parallel must not be overdrawn. The growing interdependence among countries was largely of a monetary nature in the 1930s, whereas it has much more to do with common dependence on vital resources in the 1970s. Current circumstances call for far more profound adjustments than those needed four decades ago. The need is not merely for new supranational institutions to make the international monetary and trade systems work, but for some fundamental shifts in direction. The changes lying ahead are not trivial. They challenge some of the basic values and principles underlying our existing social and economic system. Momentous decisions will be required of political leaders in the years immediately ahead.

There are numerous indications that we may be on the verge of one of the great discontinuities in human history—economic, demographic, political. The tripling of global economic activity during the third quarter of this century is not likely to be repeated during the final quarter. Stated otherwise, the global economic growth rate seems certain to slow, with the slowdown concentrated in the more affluent societies. Continuing on the present demographic path would appear to be disastrous on several counts.

As it becomes more difficult to expand supplies of certain commodities, attention is certain to focus more on distribution of available supplies, both within and among societies. Because the world is increasingly dependent on common resources, the question of how these resources are distributed among societies will loom large in the years ahead. As supply expansion becomes more costly, both ecologically and economically, emphasis will shift to demand conservation, the more efficient use of existing resources.

The difficulties inherent in attempting to expand indefinitely the supply of many resources as rapidly as the growth in demand are transforming the world markets for many raw materials from buyers' markets to sellers' markets. These changes have caused an abrupt shift in concern in international trade policy, from the traditional overriding issue of how to obtain assured access to markets abroad for whatever one exports, to the issue of assured access to raw materials needed for import. Closely related is the changing distribution of political power, moving from the historical concentration of political power in those countries which control capital and technology to a more diffuse power structure where those who control scarce raw materials will also be able to exercise considerable influence in the world's affairs. The discontinuities that are either already under way or called for suggest that it would be a serious error by economic and political decision-makers to view the final quarter of this century as merely an extrapolation of the third.

The recent writings of two very thoughtful analysts, one American and one European, reflect the sense of fundamental challenge and discontinuity now confronting the human community. Economic philosopher Robert Heilbroner wonders out loud in his new book, *An Inquiry into the Human Prospect,* whether mankind's odyssey through time may not resemble a Greek tragedy, where the hero moves toward the end he has unwittingly arranged for himself. He points out that "such a view is by no means the expression of only a few perverse minds."

Aurelio Peccei, Italian businessman and president of the Club of Rome, writing in the December 1973 issue of *Successo,* echoes a similar theme. He writes of the "events and trends that are interacting with force and speed creating situations of instability and crisis throughout the world." Peccei then points out that the inexorable development of events will compel us to make certain basic decisions that will shape the course of the future. He further recognizes that mankind as a whole will be involved in the choice, because all its components will, purposefully or unconsciously, actively or passively, contribute to it.

If, at a time of acute international stress, individual countries blame others for their problems and turn inward, then the future is not very hopeful. As of the mid-1970s, one must search for signals as to which way the international community will turn. There are a number of disturbing signs that countries, at least initially, are searching for national solutions to problems which have only global solutions. Some energy importing countries are bartering arms or exclusive economic arrangements for oil. Within the United States, in early 1974 the House of Representatives voted not to replenish the U.S. contribution to the World Bank's International Development Association, the major source of concessional capital assistance to the poorest countries. At a time of soaring food prices and acute hunger in several developing countries, the U.S. and international food assistance programs are shrinking rapidly, even though by early 1974 food riots were commonplace in a number of low-income countries, including Bolivia, Ethiopia, and India.

Not all signs are negative. Among the positive signs was a call by U.S. Secretary of State Henry Kissinger for a world food conference in 1974, following a similar call by the Conference of Nonaligned Nations in Algeria. The international community was quick to respond, and a conference was scheduled under UN auspices for November 1974 in Rome. A conference is no substitute for action, but it does constitute recognition of a problem, an essential first step for coping with it.

The year 1974 is World Population Year, and the World Population Conference is being convened in Bucharest. A World Plan of Action will be discussed. Whether one materializes and how effective it will be remain to be seen. But the fact that the two words "world" and "action" are incorporated into the same plan is a major step forward in this traditional area of controversy.

Creating a Workable World Order

The need to stabilize population sooner rather than later must not be viewed in isolation, but as part of a broader effort to create a workable world order. Such an effort must not only strive to slow population growth as rapidly as possible, but it must also seek to arrest the pursuit of superaffluence. An indefinite increase in either the number of people in the world or in the amount of goods and services consumed by each individual would eventually put unbearable stress on the earth's ecosystem and resources. If the developed countries continue the pursuit of superaffluence as they have so successfully over the past quarter century, then the world will be threatened as surely as if its population had multiplied several times.

Creating a workable world order means creating new supranational institutions to cope with emerging global problems. Following the disaster of the Depression and World War II, nations were prepared to work together to create the United Nations. New institutions were created in the monetary field, in international development, and in several functional areas such as agriculture, health, labor, and trade. During the mid-1970s, a second generation of supranational institutions is needed to cope with the problems which have arisen. These include new institutions to manage the exploitation of oceanic resources, to regulate national interventions in the global climatic system, and to regulate the activities of multinational corporations. A cooperative international effort is needed to create a world food reserve to replace the rapidly dwindling U.S. food reserves. A new effort is required in international trade, one which assures access of those in need to essential resources regardless of where they are located, just as the General Aagreement on Tarifis and Trade, created a generation ago, enlarged and assured access to markets for exports.

A workable world order will not likely evolve without a more equitable sharing of the world's resources among countries. It is no longer possible to separate efforts to stabilize population from the way in which resources are shared. A worsening global distribution of resources among countries will make it difficult to achieve a humane solution to the population problem. Widening gaps in consumption among national populations in a world of shrinking geographic distances is a formula for instability.

Creating a workable world order requires that national leaders perceive the changing relative threats to the well-being of their people. The real threats to man's future may have their origins much less in the relationship of man to man, and much more in the relationship of man to nature. If uncontrolled human fertility poses a greater threat to our future well-being than any other single factor, as many informed analysts now believe, then national governments must rethink the question of national security and the allocation of budgetary and human resources. At present, expenditures on the direct control of fertility worldwide total perhaps $3 billion per year. This compares with global military expenditures far in excess of $200 billion per year, exceeding the income of the poorest half of mankind. The question is whether leaders at the national level can perceive the changing nature of the threat to national security and well-being soon enough to achieve a more rational ordering of priorities before major global problems become unmanageable.

Because of the strong correlation between social well-being and fertility, many of the less developed countries will have to begin redesigning development strategies to focus more directly on the basic social needs of their people, particularly the poor majority. In this instance, the initiative for change and development rests with these countries themselves. Yet in many cases outsiders can play useful roles. They can help to identify world problems for political leaders and the public. Recently, development scholars and leaders have not only drawn attention to the inadequacies of many current development strategies, but have also helped make possible in many countries more open discussion of the problems and possible remedies without such talk being branded by their governments as irresponsible radicalism.

Those at the international level can also aid the search for new techniques, as was done, for example, by the Rockefeller and Ford Foundations in developing the new high-yield seeds and by the multidisciplinary teams on employment organized by the ILO and sent to such countries as Colombia, Sri Lanka, and Kenya. When a developing country is ready to act, there is a valuable opportunity for the international community to provide financial and technical support, such as the U.S. AID–financed new seeds, fertilizers, and irrigation wells that contributed to the jump in food production in Asia in the late 1960s.

There is a need for a major increase in the general flow of resources from rich countries to poor, both to help the latter achieve higher growth rates and to give them the capacity better to meet the basic needs of the poor. Though it is now clear that economic growth alone will not solve the problems in the low-income countries, neither will these problems be readily solved without higher growth rates. Quite simply, higher rates of growth make it easier for a determined government to carry out necessary reforms without major violence or extreme authoritarianism. Higher rates of growth require more machinery, raw materials, and technical know-how, all of which require foreign exchange. Thus it is no accident that most of the economic development and family planning "successes" have taken place in countries that have broad access to foreign aid, trade, and investment.

Many less developed countries can acquire some additional foreign exchange by adopting more outward-looking economic policies; however, the international economic environment frequently is no more congenial to their development than is the national environment in many countries to the poor majority of their people. Policies of developed countries and the structure of international institutions frequently discriminate, often inadvertently, against the poor countries in both trade and finance. Yet there must be major changes in the ways rich countries relate to poor countries if there is to be anything like the needed increase in the transfer of resources in the 1970s. Additional sources of foreign exchange must come from trade, investment, aid, and from such new global sources as the raw materials of the sea bed and the foreign exchange made available by the International Monetary Fund through its Special Drawing Rights.

Combined with appropriate national and international policies in the trade, monetary, and aid areas, the systematic simplification of life styles in the more affluent countries would free resources which could then be used to help the less developed countries solve their basic economic and social problems. A 10 percent reduction in beef consumption by Americans would free several million tons of grain for use in hungry countries. A reduction in the size of automobiles within the United States from large to medium or small automobiles would greatly reduce pressure on world energy supplies, making it considerably easier for the food-scarce less developed countries to obtain the enormous supplies of energy needed to expand their food output. This would be a small price to pay for the slowing of population growth and the creation of a more workable world order.

If we fail to understand and meet this challenge, we face the ominous prospect that the poorest countries will be hopelessly trapped at low levels of development because of the high prices of the energy fuels, foodstuffs, and fertilizers they must import. Under these circumstances, survival would become the overriding objective, forcing the abandonment of any hope for social and economic improvement. The scenario then unfolding in Asia, Africa, and Latin America would involve spreading food scarcity, continuously rising prices, and growing political instability. Governments would change hands with increasing frequency. Malnutrition would spread and rising death rates would begin to rise to reestablish the inevitable equilibrium between population and resources.

The encouraging thing about efforts to satisfy social needs and slow population growth is that they can reinforce each other positively. Progress made on one front enhances the prospects for progress on the other. Unfortunately, it is equally true that these two trends can reinforce each other negatively. Rapid population growth makes it more difficult to satisfy basic social needs, and this in turn hinders efforts to slow population growth. The need today is to tilt the scales in favor of the positive reinforcements.

There is no long-term middle ground between these two directions. Forces at work will move in one direction or the other. At issue is whether we have the understanding and the political will to determine which way they will move, whether we can interpret the danger signals, the handwriting on the wall, or whether our backs eventually will be pressed so tightly against the wall that we will not be able to see the handwriting, much less read it and act upon it.

A Manageable Task

The critical issue today is whether mankind can make the adjustments called for, short of catastrophe, in the limited time available. That this will be difficult, that it will put great stress on individuals, on national economic systems, and on the international political fabric there can be no doubt. But there is reason to believe that it is a manageable task.

During the quarter century now ending, there has been progress in improving the human condition. Although the income disparities among countries are far greater today than at mid-century, there has been some progress, however uneven geographically, in improving basic social conditions such as nutrition, life expectancy, infant mortality, and literacy. According to these indicators, the low-income countries of East Asia—China, the two Koreas, and Taiwan—containing close to a billion people, are now much closer to the advanced industrial societies than to those traditional societies still suffering from severe social deprivation. In Latin America, progress has been very uneven, with dramatic advances for some segments of the population, while conditions for other segments have actually worsened over the past generation. Pockets of urban affluence coexist with extensive concentrations of serious social deprivation as in northeastern Brazil, among the Andean Indians, and among the landless laborers of Mexico.

The extent of social deprivation in Asia, Africa, and Latin America is still extensive, involving enormous numbers of people. But these regions are no longer the vast areas of unrelieved hunger, malnutrition, disease, and illiteracy that they were a generation ago. Most of the severe social deprivation in the world today is concentrated in the Indian subcontinent and Africa. These are the areas where the poorest of the world's poor exist, where life expectancy is still on the average only 40 to 50 years, and where one infant in every six may die before one year of age.

On the population front, there is some small basis for encouragement. The global population growth rate probably peaked at some time in the late 1960s at just over 2 percent per year. Since then it has declined somewhat, and was in all likelihood below 1.9 percent in 1972. Preliminary data suggest it could have been closer to 1.8 percent in 1973. Fertility levels are gradually subsiding in most countries. Perhaps most significant is the fact that the long-standing trend of accelerating growth rates has not only been arrested but reversed. This provides at least some small basis for hope that substantial progress can be made in reducing fertility levels in the years immediately ahead.

There is also some basis for believing that life styles among the world's more affluent societies can be modified. Within the United States, a combination of high prices, scarce meat supplies, and a conscious decision by at least a segment of the American population to simplify life styles led to a reduction in per capita beef consumption in 1973 to 109 pounds, down from 116 pounds the year before. Again, this represented at least a temporary reversal of a long-term trend. Likewise, in the transportation field Americans were making adjustments to high prices and scarcity by reducing energy consumption. Several factors contributed to this, including lowering thermostats in homes and offices during the winter months, switching from larger to smaller automobiles, and relying much more on public transit. The $16 billion mass transit program proposed by the administration in early 1974 indicated a governmental willingness to invest in more efficient forms of transportation.

For the first time in history, the resources exist to extend the basic social benefits of modern civilization to all of mankind, creating the environment needed to slow population growth quickly. In 1950, there was only one major government significantly involved in assisting other countries with their economic and social development—the United States. During the past quarter century, it was first joined by the war-torn economies of Europe as they recovered, and then by Japan, until virtually every industrial country was providing economic and technical assistance to the less developed countries. In recent years, a number of countries which were once aid recipients have now come to rely largely on their own efforts, resources, and initiative. Some have begun to help others. Iran is assisting India; China provides assistance to several countries, mostly in Africa; Brazil is beginning to assist less fortunate neighboring countries in Latin America. The ratio is increasing between those countries able to provide economic and technical assistance and those countries with the greatest social deprivation.

In 1950, the World Bank was still a fledgling organization. Now it is a robust one, having doubled its loan activity over the past several years, and it is beginning to pioneer in loans for social programs, including education and health, nutrition, and family planning. In 1950, the regional development banks did not yet exist. Today both Asia and Latin America have very active regional development banks. Africa's is just getting under way.

One reason for crudely estimating the costs of providing literacy, maternal and child health services, and family planning services in earlier chapters was simply to recognize that the cost of meeting these basic social needs is now within reach of the international community. There are enough resources in the world to meet the basic social needs of people everywhere without reducing the quality of life for the affluent if the political will exists. And the costs are relatively trivial compared to many of the existing uses of public resources.

The changes occurring in raw materials markets, particularly for energy, augur well for the future development of some less developed countries. The combined revenue of eleven OPEC members in 1974 alone will total an estimated $85 billion. The larger of these nations, including Indonesia, Nigeria, and Iran, will easily utilize most of their oil income in internal development efforts. Five of the major oil exporters—Saudi Arabia, Kuwait, Libya, Abu Dhabi, and Qatar— have a combined population of scarcely 10 million. They may be earning more than $25 billion per year in excess of what they can usefully spend domestically, even with the most ambitious and sorely needed social programs and industrial development activities. If even a fraction of these resources could be combined with expanded aid from the industrial nations, particularly from the United States, which can easily afford to do far more, and channeled into the poorer areas of the world, there is a real possibility of eliminating much of the remaining serious social deprivation in the world within the next decade.

At mid-century, activity in the population area was almost entirely limited to rhetoric. It was being discussed in the United Nations, but action was still far in the future. Few governments had addressed the population threat. But today we find the UN deeply and increasingly involved, largely through the United Nations Fund for Population Activities. Those governments which are not at least orally committed to providing family planning services for their people form a dwindling minority.

Although the recent information on the rapidly unfolding ecological stresses and resource scarcities lead one to be pessimistic, there is reason to be hopeful. One reason for hoping that family planning rather than famine will solve the threat posed by population growth is that no government has yet used all the resources at its command in order to slow and stabilize its population. The two governments which have thus far come closest to doing this are Singapore and China. Both appear to have achieved substantial results. No country has yet begun to apply modern management techniques to family planning programs. The pill is making it immeasurably easier to control fertility, liberating women from their traditional role of child-bearing. A world population of 10 to 16 billion is not inevitable! Population growth can be brought to a standstill long before it reaches such threatening levels.

Whose Responsibility?

There has been a widespread tendency to consider the population threat as someone else's problem, someone else's responsibility. Rich countries are inclined to view population growth as a problem of the poor countries, even though the modest increases in their own popula- tions generate a grossly disproportionate share of the growing pres- sure on global resources. As observed earlier, the debate as to whether population growth or rising affluence is more responsible for our problems is wasteful of both time and human energy, a luxury our species can no longer afford. Both are responsible. We need to slow population growth and simplify life styles simultaneously.

Within national governments, it has been the usual practice to assign to the ministry of health all the responsibility for population policies and family planning programs. Within the health ministry, responsibility has often been further relegated to a group of medical doctors in the family planning division. But the population problem is too important to be left to a small medical staff within the bureauc- racy of a single ministry; it must be the concern of all branches and levels of government, including economic planners and ministries of education and information.

Even within families, men have tended to think of family planning as the responsibility of women. This must be a shared responsibility, for the simple reason that future population trends will very directly affect the future well-being and security of each of us, male or female.

And, above all, population policy must be the responsibility and a direct concern of the heads of state. If a national political leader frequently addresses the problem in public, and sets a personal exam- ple which others can follow, he or she can have a great effect on public thinking and individual attitudes. Official recognition of those who are making contributions in the family planning field can be exceedingly effective in creating the appropriate climate.

If a president, prime minister, or member of parliament has a vasectomy and announces it publicly, the attitudes toward vasecto- mies of men throughout the society will be affected. When a group of 343 prominent and rich French women signed and published a statement in 1971 indicating that they had had an illegal abortion in France, the hypocrisy of existing abortion laws was made a matter of public record. By challenging the government to prosecute them, something it was politically unwilling to do, these women were able to bring about a de facto liberalization of the abortion law.

In the final analysis, you and I are responsible for the problems mankind faces. All too often we become concerned about a major social problem but are unable to engage it effectively at the individual level. If we are genuinely concerned about population growth, we may ask ourselves some very specific questions: Does my government have an official policy of population stabilization? If it does not, what can I do to get such a policy adopted? Can I organize a like-minded group of people to work toward this objective? Should I be writing letters to editors on this matter, or to my political representatives?

Do the principal political leaders in my country understand the dynamics of population growth, that a 3 percent annual population growth rate means a nineteenfold increase in a century? In view of the gravity of the population threat, has my government systematically reviewed all its policies which bear directly or indirectly on population growth? For example, does my government have laws which restrict the sale or advertising of contraceptives? Does my government have any pro-natalist policies such as baby bonuses or preferred income tax status for large families?

If I am a young person entering the reproductive years, what is the fair and responsible thing for me to do in making childbearing decisions in terms of society, and in terms of the welfare of any child or children I might father or mother? Does my society offer young women alternative means of self-fulfillment to childbearing? If not, what can I do to further this end?

If I am in the later reproductive years and do not plan to have any more children, but expect to be sexually active, should I seek sterilization? Does the Planned Parenthood clinic in my community in Bangkok, Mexico City, or Detroit need volunteers to serve as receptionists or aides to doctors, or to assist with the office work? Can I help out with the fund-raising efforts, both local and international, required if family planning services are to become universally available?

Am I consuming more food or energy than I need? Can I reduce my consumption of material goods without significantly reducing my well-being? Can I donate the resultant savings to organizations providing family planning services, such as the International Planned Parenthood Federation in London? Or to a national organization doing educational work, such as Zero Population Growth within the United States?

The Role of Communications Media

As we examine the need for the vast increase in understanding and the far-reaching changes in attitudes toward childbearing and life styles which must take place in every society in the years immediately ahead, it becomes clear that the communications media have a major responsibility. Traditionally, the educational system would have been primarily responsible for changing social attitudes on such central issues as family planning and life styles. But the deadlines with which humanity is faced are so imminent that we cannot wait for this change in values to work its way through the educational system. There is not time for a generation of teachers to be trained, and for these in turn to train a generation of children who will eventually enter the child-bearing ages. The role of the educational system continues to be important, but it cannot play the central role in the crucial period between now and the end of the twentieth century.

The changes required, not only in attitudes but in practices, must occur within a matter of years. If we delay, then the issue will have been decided by inertia and against the future interests of our children and grandchildren. Mankind will already be in the process of committing demographic suicide, creating a world for which our grandchildren will curse us.

One of the urgent responsibilities of the communications media is to distinguish between symptoms and causes of the problems we face. There is a need to establish the direct linkage between population growth and its many symptoms—traffic congestion, pollution, resource scarcity, rising prices, and malnutrition. The relationship between our attitudes toward childbearing and the quality of our day-to-day existence needs to be made much clearer to each individual than it now is.

There is a pressing requirement to increase understanding of the nature of exponential growth. Relatively few people, even among those of us with advanced formal education, understand that a seemingly innocuous growth rate of 3 percent per year results in a nineteen-fold increase within a century. This simple fact needs to be repeated again and again until it permeates the consciousness of people everywhere, from national policy-makers to every individual couple contemplating another child.

The role of the communications media is a dual one: (1) to dramatize the reality of the population threat and the need to reduce births; and (2) to provide practical guidance on how to reduce births. The communications media are in a unique position to help us all, literate or illiterate, to understand the full consequences of continuing population growth as it affects individual well-being, security, and life styles. Television, in particular, can demonstrate the relationship of population growth to ecological stresses and resource scarcity. People need to be informed as to the kinds of behavioral change required to cope with global ecological stresses and resource scarcities, and not only in the adoption of family planning practices but also in the simplification of life styles. Parents and prospective parents everywhere should be acquainted with the results of the exceedingly valuable demographic and medical research undertaken in recent years on the benefits of planning families, particularly on the relationship between family size and spacing of children and the health of both mother and infant. Above all, there is a need for practical information on the local availability of family planning services, including contraceptive supplies.

One of the few bright spots in the current situation is the capacity of the communications media to mobilize people and resources, to inform and thereby shape public opinion, and to help to transform societies. This capacity is far greater today than it has ever been in the past, and it will be even greater in the future. The media must accept new responsibilities for the education of an audience ranging from illiterate farmers in village societies to housewives in industrial suburbs.

The ubiquitous transistor radio can become an instrument of social reform in less developed countries if properly used. The village television set has an enormous educational potential. Whether or not this potential is fully realized depends almost entirely on the programming available. As literacy levels rise, newspapers and periodicals become increasingly important as a means of disseminating information and understanding of the challenges humanity confronts. But the basic task, especially in the less developed countries and among the lower economic and social strata in more developed nations, will fall on television and radio for the years immediately ahead.

Toward a New Social Ethic

A social ethic is a set of principles, a code of behavior that enables society to function and survive. The social ethic that now guides mankind in matters of childbearing, the production and distribution of wealth, and the relationship of man to nature is one which has evolved over the millennia. By and large, it has served us well. Not only have we survived as a species, but we have greatly multiplied our numbers and in some instances prospered as well. But now the old ethic is no longer adequate. Some values must be modified or abandoned, others strengthened, adjusting to the discontinuities now confronting us. The crucial factor may not be the required changes themselves but the limited time available for man to accept and adapt to them.

Changes in attitudes and values are required of people everywhere. The needed changes may far exceed those any earlier generation has been called upon to make. One of the basic tenets underlying modern societies has been that man should have dominion over nature, subjugating the environment to his needs. It is this tenet which is partly responsible for the worsening environmental crisis. The new ethic must encompass a new naturalism that places greater emphasis on man's harmony with nature and less on his dominance over it.

In seeking a more harmonious relationship with nature, our emerging global society will have to formulate a new childbearing ethic. Throughout most of man's existence, large numbers of children were necessary to ensure survival of the species, given the high infant and child death rates. Now that today's birth rates threaten the very life-support systems on which man depends, man must abandon the old "be fruitful and multiply" ethic, replacing it with one designed to stabilize population.

Conditions are now forcing us to distinguish between responsible adulthood and parenthood. Being adult with all it implies for mature and responsible behavior may no longer lead us toward parenthood. The new ethic must see men and women as socially equal, with childbearing not an automatically assumed function but an option which women may or may not pursue, according to their personal dictates.

Another central component in the existing ethic is a near exclusive emphasis on production and on the acquisition of wealth as an end in itself. A by-product of thousands of years of material scarcity, this preoccupation must give way to a much greater emphasis on distribution and sharing. The existence of widespread global poverty in the late twentieth century is not a result of a lack of technology to raise individual productivity but the lack of attention given to the diffusion of technology and wealth on a global scale. Modern man has excelled at production but failed at distribution.

Extreme emphasis on superaffluence has no place in an ecosystem already under great stress at existing levels of economic activity. Circumstances require that nations give up outdated notions of independence and sovereignty, replacing conflict and competition with cooperation against the shared perils of the human race. The need for a new ethic is no longer in doubt. It should not be a culturally biased ethic, but a universal one, a response to the circumstances in which man finds himself in the twentieth century. Such an ethic would have far-reaching implications for the behavior of both individuals and national governments. There is no denying that it would result in new life styles and a global society far different from the one we now know.

The Need for Leadership

The changes called for in human values and behavior and in institutions of all types during the final quarter of the twentieth century are without precedent. The historical equivalent of perhaps two centuries of change in values and behavior must be compressed into a generation. Under these circumstances, the world faces a desperate need for leadership at all levels. There are many scarce commodities today, but none as scarce as leadership.

We seek national solutions to national problems when the only feasible solutions are international, or in some cases global. Efforts to provide national solutions may only frustrate efforts to find workable solutions. Our emerging problems call for highly sophisticated understanding, but a lack of understanding is evident at all levels. We confuse symptoms of problems with causes, often treating the symptoms and in the process further aggravating the problem. All too often we research and seek narrow solutions to problems within individual disciplines—engineering, economics, or ecology—when most of the important problems mankind faces no longer fit neatly into the academic departments of universities or the agencies of government.

The world desperately needs enlightened leadership from national political leaders, corporate leaders, church leaders, UN civil servants, labor unions, and citizen groups. But enlightened leaders are few. Leadership at the national level is particularly critical, and yet few national leaders have access to the information needed for responsible and intelligent decision-making in many critical areas. National officeholders will be under great pressure to provide leadership of the caliber the times call for. It will not be easy. There will be a great temptation to dodge critical issues, to blame other countries for problems which were not anticipated. More than anything else, the times call for political leaders who can behave like statesmen, and for informed, concerned citizens who make it good politics for them to do so.

Suggested Readings

Berelson, Bernard, ed. *World Population: Status Report 1974; A Guide for the Concerned Citizen*. Population Council, *Reports on Population/Family Planning*, January 1974.

Berg, Alan, portions with Robert J. Muscat. *The Nutrition Factor: Its Role in National Development*. Washington, D.C.: Brookings Institution, 1973.

Brown, Lester R. *Seeds of Change: The Green Revolution and Development in the 1970s*. New York: Praeger Publishers, 1970.

———. *World without Borders*. New York: Random House, 1972.

Bryant, John. *Health and the Developing World*. Ithaca, N.Y.: Cornell University Press, 1969.

Critchfield, Richard. *The Golden Bowl Be Broken: Peasant Life in Four Cultures*. Bloomington, Ind.: Indiana University Press, 1973.

Curry-Lindahl, Kai. *Let Them Live: A Worldwide Survey of Animals Threatened with Extinction*. New York: William Morrow and Company, 1972.

Ehrlich, Paul R., and Anne H. Ehrlich. *Population, Resources, Environment: Issues in Human Ecology*, rev. ed. San Francisco: W. H. Freeman and Company, 1972

Falk, Richard A. *This Endangered Planet: Prospects and Proposals for Human Surival*. New York: Random House, 1971.

Frejka, Tomas. *The Future of Population Growth: Alternative Paths to Equilibrium*. A Population Council Book. New York: John Wiley and Sons, 1973.

Grant, James P. *Growth from Below: A People-Oriented Development Strategy*. Development Paper 16. Overseas Development Council, 1973.

———. "Marginal Men: The Global Unemployment Crisis," *Foreign Affairs*, vol. 50, no. 1 (October 1971).

Heilbroner, Robert. *An Inquiry into the Human Prospect*. New York: W. W. Norton and Company, 1974.

Idyll, C. P. "The Anchovy Crisis." *Scientific American*, vol. 228, no. 6 (June 1973).

Inadvertent Climate Modification: Report of the Study of Man's Impact on Climate (SMIC). Cambridge, Mass.: MIT Press, 1971.

International Labor Office. *Towards Full Employment: A Program for Colombia*. Geneva, 1970.

———. *Matching Employment Opportunities and Expectations: A Program of Action for Ceylon*. Geneva, 1971.

———. *Employment, Incomes, and Equality: A Strategy for Increasing Productive Employment in Kenya.* Geneva, 1972.

Kocher, James E. *Rural Development, Income Distribution, and Fertility Decline.* New York: Population Council, 1973

Lapp, Ralph E. *The Logarithmic Century: Charting Future Shock.* Englewood Cliffs, N.J.: Prentice-Hall, Inc., 1973.

Lovins, Amory. "Population and Natural Resources: Energy Resources." Submitted to UN ECOSOC Symposium on Population, Resources, and Environment, Stockholm, 26 September–5 October 1973. E/Conf. 60/SYM. III/12, 5 September 1973.

McDonald, J. Corbett. *Unmet Needs in Family Planning.* London: International Planned Parenthood Federation, 1973.

McNamara, Robert S. *One Hundred Countries, Two Billion People: The Dimensions of Development.* New York: Praeger Publishers, 1973.

Man's Impact on the Global Environment: Assessment and Recommendations for Action. Report of the Study of Critical Environmental Problems, sponsored by Massachusetts Institute of Technology. Cambridge, Mass.: MIT Press, 1970.

Meadows, Donella H., Dennis L. Meadows, Jørgen Randers, and William W. Behrens III. *The Limits to Growth.* A Potomac Associates Book. New York: Universe Books, 1972.

Moraes, Dom. *A Matter of People.* New York: Praeger Publishers, in cooperation with the United Nations Fund for Population Activities, 1974.

National Academy of Sciences. *Weather and Climate Modification: Problems and Progress.* Washington, D.C., 1973.

Nortman, Dorothy, assisted by Ellen Hofstatter. "Population and Family Planning: A Factbook." Population Council, *Reports on Population/Family Planning,* 5th ed., no. 2, September 1973.

Olson, Mancur, and Hans H. Landsberg, eds. *The No-Growth Society. Daedalus,* vol. 102, no. 4 (Fall 1973), the American Academy of Arts and Sciences.

Overseas Development Council. *The United States and the Developing World: Agenda for Action, 1974.* New York: Praeger Publishers, 1974.

Owens, Edgar, and Robert Shaw. *Development Reconsidered.* Lexington, Mass.: Lexington Books, 1972.

Partan, Daniel G. *Population in the United Nations System: Developing the Legal Capacity and Programs of UN Agencies.* Law and Population Book series, no. 3. Durham, N.C.: Rule of Law Press, 1973.

Peccei, Aurelio. "The Moment of Truth Is Approaching." *Successo,* December 1973, pp. 109–20.

Piotrow, Phyllis T. *World Population Crisis: The United States Response.* New York: Praeger Publishers, 1973.

Population and the American Future. Report of the Commission on Population Growth and the American Future. New York: New American Library, 1972.

Rich, William. *Smaller Families through Social and Economic Progress.* Monograph no. 7. Washington, D.C.: Overseas Development Council, 1973.

Taylor, Howard C. and Bernard Berelson. "Comprehensive Family Planning Based on Maternal/Child Health Services: A Feasibility Study for a World Program." Population Council, *Studies in Family Planning,* vol. 2, no. 2 (February 1971).

Turnham, David, and Ingelies Jaeger. *The Employment Problem in Less Developed Countries: A Review of the Evidence.* Paris: OECD Development Center, 1970.

United Nations Secretariat. *World and Regional Population Prospects* (preliminary text). World Population Conference, 1974. E/Conf. 60/BP/3, 31 March 1973, and *Addendum: World Population Prospects beyond the Year 2000* (preliminary text), E/Conf. 60/BP/3/Add. 1, 16 May 1973.

U.S. Agency for International Development, Office of Population. *Desert Encroachment on Arable Lands: Significance, Causes, and Control.* TA/OST 72–10, Washington, D.C., August 1972.

Ward, Barbara, and René Dubos. *Only One Earth: The Care and Maintenance of a Small Planet.* New York: W. W. Norton and Company, 1972.